W9-BOB-006

From Earthquakes to Global Unity

The End Times Have Begun

by Paul McGuire

Huntington House Publishers

Copyright © 1996
All rights reserved. No part of this book may be
reproduced without permission from the publisher,
except by a reviewer who may quote brief passages in
a review; nor may any part of this book be reproduced, stored in a retrieval system or copied by me-
chanical photocopying, recording or other means,
without permission from the publisher.

Huntington House Publishers
P.O. Box 53788
Lafayette, Louisiana 70505

Library of Congress Card Catalog Number 95-78183
ISBN 1-56384-107-X

Unless otherwise indicated
all Scripture quotations are taken from the
Holy Bible, New King James Version,
copyright 1982 by Thomas Nelson, Inc.

Printed in the U.S.A.

Contents

Chapter One

What on Earth Is Happening?

We are in a period like no other in the history of mankind. There are political, economic, and social forces at work which have the capacity to radically change the landscape of our society, nation, and world. On an almost daily basis, through satellite and television, we now have the power to witness instantaneously events that go on around the world. Images of riots, earthquakes, wars, murders, and social upheaval pour into our living rooms.

Over a quarter of a century ago, the brilliant futurist Alvin Toffler wrote the book *Future Shock* to outline the overwhelming changes that were happening to our society. But, today as we race towards the new millennium, we have gone beyond shock into a kind of sensory overload. With stroboscopic intensity our minds are filled with media images of the horrible bombing of the Oklahoma City federal building, the Japanese subway victims who were gassed by a doomsday cult, the incredible devastation of earthquakes, and armed conflicts in remote regions of the world.

Our television screens blare with scenes of blue helmeted U.N. troops invading nations like Haiti, Somalia, Rwanda, and the coming computerized banking cards that will move us into a cashless society. Talks about a new Middle East and peace talks between Israel and her Arab neighbors seem to play out a scenario mapped out centuries ago by the ancient Hebrew prophets. It appears that we are in what only could be described as a count-down to the end of the world. It could be that we are on the very edge of Armageddon.

Significant Factors

I was talking with a friend the other day about biblical prophecies concerning the end of the world, the Rapture of the Church, and the coming one-world government. I remarked to him that there are significant factors point-ing to the fact that we are entering a period of fulfillment of biblical prophecy. For example, it is no accident that Israel was reformed as a nation in 1948 by the United Nations and that since that time there has been an explo-sion in world evangelism.

In addition, there are powerful organizations like the Trilateral Commission, the Council on Foreign Relations, and the United Nations that are pushing for a new world order that may be a fulfillment of what the prophet Daniel warned about centuries ago. At the same time, over one million Smart Cards will be released this year. These Smart Cards will have tiny microchips containing biographical data, credit information, and available bank funds which can be interconnected to a national computer system. Over one million of these Smart Cards will be released in the United States this year as a test for the coming cash-less society.

Our president continues to place United States troops under the command of U.N. foreign military officers. In fact, even as you read these words, U.S. troops have been deployed as United Nations troops in over one hundred nations of the world.

On the cultural level we are seeing widespread immo-rality, such as hard core pornography, which is pumped into so-called normal middle class homes through cable television and is available in practically every hotel in America. Hollywood uses its electronic soap box of films, videos, and television to preach to us the virtues of the homosexual lifestyle, casual sex, abortion rights, and the gospel of tolerance, which basically says anything goes.

Despite the great strides the men's movement has made in our nation, most American companies encourage males to be "married to the company," and the lack of committed fathers along with the continued breakup of families has produced several generations of young people with deep-seated psychological problems. The decline of the traditional family has contributed to the increase in violent crime, rape, incest, alcoholism, drug use, and suicide.

As the family unit continues to deteriorate, a new breed of social engineers has arisen to replace the family with the government and has suggested that we now "license" parents and establish the United Nations Rights of the Child, which strips parents of their authority to raise their children without government interference.

The optimism of the 1950s which believed that man could accomplish anything through technology is fading into despair and pessimism as we approach the next millennium. No longer are drugs like antibiotics the miracle cures they were a generation ago as new strains of tuberculosis, pneumonia, the deadly Ebola virus, and "flesh eating" diseases have emerged in a state of outbreak in our world. The AIDS epidemic is sweeping the world, and millions are projected to die in the next decade.

Even the very ground we are standing on is shaken as earthquakes rock our world from Northridge, California, to Kobe, Japan. To top it all off, global weather patterns seem to be changing, and we are seeing an increase in both flooding and droughts around the world. Scientists appear to be totally baffled as some declare we are entering a period of global warming and others suggest that we are in a new ice age.

Global terrorism and acts of senseless violence are on the increase. The devastating images of a government building in Oklahoma City being ripped apart by a bomb four times as powerful as the one set off at the World Trade Center are a painful reminder of the evil and cruelty that exist in our world. The seeds of hatred that were sown in the hearts of our own "homegrown American terrorists" erupted into a holocaust of dead bodies and devastation.

If all these sociological, political, and environmental events were isolated, there would be perhaps no cause for alarm. But, since these events are increasing in intensity and happening all at the same time, it could be that we are witnessing the "signs of the times at the end of the age" spoken of by Jesus Christ in Matthew, chapter 24.

Finally, the rapid spread of militant Islamic fundamentalism and the fact that Russia is selling nuclear materials to nations like Iran is an indication that we could be nearing the massive invasion of Israel that is detailed in Ezekiel 38 and 39. This war of Gog and Magog against Israel is what many believe is the beginning of the Armageddon, which will happen before Jesus Christ returns to this earth and sets up His millennial kingdom.

If these things were happening individually, we would still be concerned, but they are happening collectively and have been increasing in intensity since 1948 when Israel was reformed as a nation. Even the most skeptical observer would have to acknowledge that the likelihood of all these events happening at the same time accidently or randomly is highly improbable.

It is truly remarkable that so many of the ancient biblical prophecies are happening at the same time with increasing intensity. I believe that we are on the threshold of the greatest global change the world has ever seen. I have spent decades researching sociological, political, and spiritual trends, yet it has only been through my study of the Bible that I have been truly able to understand current events. In the following pages, I have attempted to outline possible prophetic scenarios that could happen in the near future. I believe that, for believers in

Jesus Christ, we are about to embark on the greatest adventure in the history of the human race. At the same time, I look with deep sadness at the billions of people who are alive on planet earth who do not know the Savior—the Messiah Jesus Christ.

In the time that God has given me on this earth I want to do everything possible to share with others that reality of God's existence and that Jesus Christ spilled His blood so that they might live forever with Him in eternity. I have learned that a lot of people have no desire to enter a church, and yet many people are fascinated by how Bible prophecy applies to current events. It is my prayer that this book can be used in part as a bridge to people who do not know God.

I have attempted to map out some possible scenarios based on my study of current events and the truth of God's Word. I do not claim some special revelation from God or to have seen a vision of the end times as John did in the Book of Revelation. This book is merely an attempt to examine possible future events as they apply to the Scriptures. As you read these pages, it is my hope that you will discover how the ancient biblical prophets speak today and that you will seek a closer relationship with Jesus Christ.

You Don't Need a Weatherman to Know Which Way the Wind Blows

The old Bob Dylan song had the lyrics, "You don't need a weatherman to know which way the wind blows." Clearly, our world is on the very brink of massive global change. There are powerful economic, political, and spiritual forces which are going to radically transform the very nature of civilization.

It is not an accident that the powerful men who control multinational corporations are moving our world into a global society that will at some point in the future be controlled by some form of one-world government. The driving force behind the push towards global government is the endless quest for bigger monetary profits and the fear of nuclear holocaust and terrorism.

If you add technology into the mix and the advent of the new superhigh-speed computers, you begin to see that a global economic, spiritual, political infrastructure is inevitable. Manufacturing, stock markets, the threat of nuclear terrorism, communications technology, and cultural forces are forcing the demise of the individual nation-state in favor of a one-world government.

Although it is impossible to predict when this may happen, many Bible scholars believe that this coming one-world government is going to be taken over by a charismatic world leader the Bible calls the Anti-christ. Jesus Christ spoke of this countdown period to the end of the age and what He called the "abomination of desolation" in Matthew, chapters 24 and 25. He compared these massive societal and global changes to a woman in the early stages of childbirth. Our planet is experiencing the first contractions of a brand new world, and it is important that we recognize the signs of the times.

No one knows the exact timing of these things but God Himself. And, there is a great danger in assigning dates and specific timetables to end-time events. Many people have discredited the truth of the gospel of Jesus Christ and the integrity of Bible prophecy by saying that Adolf Hitler, Mussolini, and even Henry Kissinger are the Anti-christ. This kind of careless and foolish speculation has discredited the legitimate prophecies in the Bible.

After the Oklahoma City bombing there has been a concerted effort in the mainstream media to label anyone who is concerned about a one-world government as paranoid and a right-wing extremist. Peter Jennings of ABC News said anybody who is talking about the Anti-christ and a new world government was part of this right-wing extremist movement. Yet, the subject of the coming new world order has been talked about by men like former President George Bush and Pope John Paul, II.

Without question there have been some pretty wild conspiracy theories that have been circulating, and there is a lunatic fringe out there that is dangerous. But, to put all law-abiding and tax-paying citizens who express legitimate concerns about growth of government and the role of organizations like the United Nations and the Council on Foreign Relations in the same camp with these dangerous groups is manipulative and dishonest. During the last fifty years there have been countless mainstream political leaders who have voiced publicly their concerns about such matters.

The mass media has literally had a feeding frenzy around the word *conspiracy*. However, the really big conspiracy is bigger than anything in this physical world. I believe that the ultimate conspiracy is not on the earthly level but in the spiritual world or invisible realm.

In Ephesians 6:12, the Apostle Paul reveals the true conspiracy that we are struggling against when he says, "For we do not wrestle against flesh and blood, but against principalities, against powers, against the rulers of the darkness of this age, against spiritual hosts of wickedness in the heavenly places." This ultimate conspiracy is not an earthly one, but a cosmic conspiracy. In this conspiracy, men, human governments, and other organizations can become pawns of dark supernatural powers that seek to enslave mankind and prepare the world for the coming of the Anti-christ.

Eschatology: The Doctrine of Last Things

In modern society, people want to know the bottom line and what's really going on. In addition, modern man has an enormous fascination with the future. This is the reason movies like the *Star Trek* series and other science fiction films do so well. In the study of the Bible there is eschatology, which comes from the Greek word *eschatos* meaning "last" and *logos* which means "subject matter." Eschatology is the study which deals with the last events in human history.

Eschatology deals with events like the Second Coming of Jesus Christ, the time of His coming, the signs of His coming, the Rapture of the Church, the Tribulation, the Anti-christ, the Resurrection, the Millennium, Israel, Satan and fallen angels, the future destiny of those who reject Jesus Christ, heaven, and the future of those who have accepted Jesus Christ as their Lord and Savior.

Eschatology is that aspect of biblical doctrine which deals with the end times or "last things." Even the Apostle John believed that he was living in the last hour when he said in 1 John 2:18, "Little children, it is the last hour; and as you have heard that the Anti-christ is coming, even now many Anti-christs have come, by which we know it is the last hour."

In Matthew 25:1–13 and 2 Timothy 4:8, we are taught to actively expect the return of Jesus Christ. Matthew 25:1–13 states,

> Then the kingdom of heaven shall be likened to ten virgins who took their lamps and went out to meet their bridegroom. Now five of them were wise, and five were foolish. Those who were foolish took their lamps and no oil with them, but the wise took oil in their vessels with their lamps. But while the bridegroom was delayed, they all slumbered and slept. And at midnight a cry was heard: "Behold, the bridegroom is coming go out to meet him!" Then those virgins arose and trimmed their lamps. And the foolish said to the wise, "Give us some of your oil, for our lamps are going out." But the wise answered, saying "No, lest there should be not enough for us and you: but go rather to those who sell and buy for yourselves." And while they went to buy, the bridegroom came, and those who were ready went in with him to the wedding; and the door was shut. Afterward the other virgins came also, saying "Lord, Lord open to us!" But he answered and said, "Assuredly, I say to you, I do not know you." Watch therefore, for you know neither

the day nor the hour in which the Son of Man is coming.

In 2 Timothy 4:8 it states, "Finally, there is laid up for me the crown of righteousness, which the Lord, the righteous Judge, will give to me on that Day, and not to me only but also to all those who have loved his appearing." God is trying to cultivate an attitude in His people to expect the return of His Son Jesus Christ.

Chapter Two

Whole Lot of Shaking Going On

I t was around 4:00 A.M. in our home in northern Los Angeles County. My wife had gotten up because she couldn't sleep and was in the process of going through some files. She was upstairs and I thought I heard her drop a large box. Quite frankly, I was beginning to get irritated because she was making so much noise so early in the morning.

However, those thoughts had not even passed through my mind when it sounded as if she had dropped a whole truckload of boxes. At that very second, the house began to shake so violently that my first thought was that a thermonuclear weapon had gone off, and we had just been hit by the blast.

All of my thoughts were split-second pulses of disoriented reason as the next thirty seconds seemed like an hour. Since I had been in southern California for almost two decades, I did not think this was an earthquake. Yet, the house began to shake so violently that I thought the roof was going to cave-in any second, and I was preparing to run upstairs to grab my children. However, I was being thrown around the room. In another pulse-like thought I realized this was a massive earthquake on a scale I had never dreamed of.

It was like being stuck in the Stephen Speilberg movie *Close Encounters of the Third Kind*. Then, in a second, it resided, and I shouted with all my strength to my wife upstairs, "Grab the kids!" Yet, like a fearless bionic woman mobilized by the chemical fury of a super-adrenaline high, the kind that only a total crisis can bring on, she had grabbed all three of our young children and was heading down the stairs where she met me; I grabbed two children, and we bolted from the house.

We headed for the driveway to scramble for safety. As we shivered together outside, suddenly all the lights of the city went out, and our neighbors began to run out of their houses. I was shivering in a T-shirt and underwear when the night sky became a dark blue and a billion bright stars appeared now that the light of the city had gone out.

It was a strange feeling to stand there in the aftermath of a massive earthquake and to see the night stars brighter than I had ever seen them. There, with civilization eclipsed, the great expanse of the universe overshadowed us. Moments later there were about fifty neighbors huddled in blankets on our driveway waiting in terrified anticipation as the aftershocks continued. A car radio blasted the news in the night that the city had just experienced a powerful 6.7 earthquake that had plunged Los Angeles into total darkness. One Hollywood comedian described his experience of going through the Northridge earthquake like "waking up in a blending machine drunk" because the early morning shaking was so violent and unexpected.

For the next week, we lived in tents outside of our homes with power, water, and heat cut off. Our lives were forever changed as we were cut off from the rest of Los Angeles due to freeway collapses, and we found ourselves driving four-hour commutes each way on winding mountain roads.

The system had completely broken down in a cataclysmic upheaval brought about by a major natural disaster which made it seem like it was the end of the world. What we learned in the next few weeks and months is how quickly our life can be changed forever in an instant and just how fragile all of our life systems are even here in America. Food, water, electricity, heat, shelter, clothing banks, jobs, and safety can be stopped in a heartbeat. The entire socioeconomic system upon which we base our lives can literally vanish in moments.

Here in America we seem to think that we are immune from the kind of disasters we read about on a global scale. We naively think that our systems will hold and our man-centered institutions will prevail even in the midst of calamity. Yet, as a society and as individuals we skate on a thin veneer of ice with which the slightest increase in weight can send us crashing to our destruction.

What happened in southern California in the Northridge earthquake was just a microcosm of what can happen in an instant to our society and world when forces outside of our control, either natural or social, go out of control. With the rise of natural disasters such as earthquakes, hurricanes, floods and the increase of wars, famines, and plagues, our lonely little planet called earth appears to be on either the eve of destruction or the birth of a brand new world.

In the New Testament Jesus Christ told his disciples "the signs of the times at the end of the age" when he said:

> For many will come in My name, saying, "I am the Christ," and will deceive many. And you will hear of wars and rumors of wars. See that you are not troubled: for all these must come to pass, but the end is not yet. For nation will rise against nation, and kingdom against kingdom. And there will be famines, pestilences, and earthquakes in various places. All these are the beginning of sorrows. Then they will deliver you up to tribulation and kill you, and you will be hated by all nations for My name's sake. And many will be offended, will betray one another, and will hate one another. Then many false prophets will rise up and deceive many. And because lawlessness will abound the love of many

will grow cold. But he who endures to the end shall
be saved. And this gospel of the kingdom will be
preached in all the world as a witness to all the
nations, and then the end will come. (Matt. 24:5–
14)

The words of Jesus Christ describe with remarkable accuracy the social condition of our world. In fact, today's
newspaper headlines could come right out of the Bible as
we see the ancient prophetic scenario unfold before our
very eyes.

David Koresh in Waco, Texas; the Northridge earthquake; AIDs; drive-by shootings; the breakdown of the
Soviet Empire and it's resulting wars; the increasing hostility by the mass media and many members of our society to biblical values; famines in Africa and other nations;
and the global presentation of the gospel of Jesus Christ
all describe what Jesus Christ talked about when He described the "signs of the times and the end of the age."

Ring of Fire

Again in Matthew 24:7 Jesus warned, "And there will
be famines, pestilences and earthquakes in various places."
During the last year there were over a dozen earthquakes
of the 5.0 magnitude in the Pacific Rim in a region that
is called the Ring of Fire. California has received several
earthquakes after the Northridge one and a recent one of
5.0 on the Richter scale near Sacramento.

Japan had its largest earthquake in over twenty-five
years which measured 7.9, and the quake caused major
aftershocks in Taiwan. On 8 June an earthquake happened four hundred miles under the surface of Bolivia
and was felt as far away as the United States and Canada.
Papua, New Guinea, which is also along the Ring of Fire,
experienced a 5.1 quake which caused major volcanic
eruptions.

The Big One

A 7.2 earthquake rocked Kobe, Japan, and killed over forty-eight hundred people and destroyed twenty-one hundred buildings. The quake, which rocked buildings forty miles away, hit at daybreak like the Northridge quake and derailed trains, collapsed freeways, spread fires, and created cataclysmic devastation.

Japan has had a history of earthquakes in this century. Starting in 1923, a Tokyo earthquake of magnitude 8.3 killed one hundred thousand people, and they have had numerous earthquakes since then. All this seismic activity has caused scientists in California to issue new findings. Scientific teams at Caltech, University of Southern California, and the U.S. Geological Survey believe that southern California is due for the "Big One," which they believe will be a powerful earthquake of the 7.2 to 7.6 magnitude. According to these scientists a 7.0 earthquake could easily topple a twenty-story building ("Seismic Forecast: Shaky Future or a False Alarm," *Los Angeles Times*, 17 January 1995, B12).

Nature Out of Control

In Matthew 24:7–8, Jesus Christ related to His disciples signs of His Second Coming. He said, "For nation will rise up against nation, and kingdom against kingdom. And there will be famines, pestilences, and earthquakes in various places. All these are the beginning of sorrows." And, in the Old Testament the ancient Jews knew that there was a direct relationship between favorable weather and the blessing of God on their lives. In Deuteronomy, chapter 28, there is an outline of their covenant with God which promised blessings in all areas of their lives and an entire list of curses if they followed idols and disobeyed their God.

In 1993 *Life* magazine documented the record weather damage in the United States. There were a record 1,297 tornadoes in 1993; a Boise National Forest fire that destroyed three thousand acres; the fires in southern California that destroyed thousands of acres from Malibu to Orange County; and the Mississippi-Missouri flood, which caused over $25 billion in damage. On 15 June 1991, the eruption of Mount Pinatubo in the Philippines was the greatest shock to the earth's biosphere in over one hundred years; it was caused by massive rains penetrating the earth's surface and touching off volcanic activity. The explosion was so great that it actually lowered the earth's weather by one degree Fahrenheit, and many meteorologists think that there is a relationship between the Midwest flooding and the drought in the southeastern United States and the Pinatubo explosion.

The 1994 Northridge earthquake, which could total $40 billion in damage, has been called the largest natural disaster in U.S. history. Although, I do not believe that God is sending these disasters upon us. I do think the Bible gives a direct relationship between a society's spiritual condition and divine protection. If a nation shakes its fist at God, which our nation has done by slaughtering a million babies a year through abortion, it is possible that God removes His protective hand and allows nature to take over. Clearly, God intends to protect His people and the innocent but a shaking occurs, which is used by God to awaken people to their need for Him.

It is interesting to note that the Northridge earthquake epicenter was the very heart of the global pornography business where the majority of the nation's X-rated films are produced. Again, I do not believe that it was God sending an earthquake, but when a nation wants nothing to do with God, I think He honors that request and removes His hand of protection. Perhaps, the only thing preventing massive destruction in the United States is the existence of God's people, His desire to save the lost, His mercy, and the fact that the United States is still the center of global missionary activity.

A New Ice Age

Although major U.S. news magazines, Vice Pres. Al Gore, and the radical ecological movement have been warning us about the dangers of global warming, the scientific reality is that we are either in or about to experience the effects of a brand new ice age. According to Laurence Hecht writing for *Twenty-first Century Science & Technology* ("The Coming [or Present] Ice Age," Winter 1993–1994, 23), "We are now in an ice age and have been for about the past 2 million years." All the latest scientific evidence totally contradicts the global warming theory upon which much of the ecological movement is built. Hecht warns concerning the global warming theory, "this is not science but intellectual dishonesty bordering on fraud."

Not only is the earth not getting warmer, it is actually getting colder. However, the danger is that, as the earth continues on in a new ice age, we may expect to see the following conditions that happened during a five-hundred year period of extreme cooling called the Little Ice Age which from 1550 to as late as 1813 produced:

• increasing frequency of freezing rivers and lakes;
• increasing severity of windstorms and sea floods;
• harvest failures and rising prices of wheat and bread;
• abandonment of tillage, vineyards, and farm villages;
• increased incidence of disease and death among human and animal populations.

Chapter Three

The Days of Noah

I n Matthew 24:37–39 Jesus Christ said, "But as the days of Noah were, so also will the coming of the Son of Man be. For in the days before the flood, they were eating and drinking, marrying and giving in marriage, until the day that Noah entered the ark, and did not know until the flood came and took them all away, so also will the coming of the Son of Man be." Can you imagine Noah's neighbors sitting around drinking margaritas and having barbecues while he built the ark? Just picture the neighbors' reaction as Noah left the ark in the driveway for about a year before the floods finally came. They probably thought he was a total lunatic and a religious fanatic. Then, one day the flood came and drowned them all while Noah and his family floated to safety on the ark.

Jesus Christ said that when He returns people are going to have the same mindset. Just look at what is happening today. All across this planet there are signs of the times which are signaling the real possibility that Jesus may be coming soon. Yet, people continue to laugh at that fact, party, get married, and live as if nothing was going to happen. According to *U.S. News & World Report*, 40 to 60 percent of Americans pay some attention to a belief in biblical prophecy ("The Faces of Doomsday," *U.S. News & World Report* [19 October 1992]: 73). Yet, the vast majority of Americans are not living lives that are pleasing to God, and they are not preparing spiritually for His return.

When you drive down the freeways of southern California you see signs on peoples' cars that mock the Christian fish symbol. One of these signs is a shark and the other has the word *Darwin* in it which suggests that God did not create man but that we are evolved. If you walk into most videocassette stores or "minimarts," you will see pornography readily available. Or, just turn on your television and you will see endless violence, sex, and programs like "The Other Side" which deal with the occult. Truly America is not ready for the return of Jesus Christ. They are like the people of Noah's day who ignored the warning and their impending doom.

Genesis 6:5 states, "Then the Lord saw that the wickedness of man was great in the earth, and that every intent of the thoughts of his heart was only evil continually." This is very much like our society which is drowning in a sea of immorality, greed, perversion, violence, corruption, lies, deception, and evil. However, before the destruction and judgment came God rescued His people who were in a blood covenant relationship with Him. Noah and his family were saved from judgment by a loving God who was committed to them. In the same way, this loving God will save His people today who are in a blood covenant relationship with Him through Jesus Christ. God promises to rapture His people from the earth before His wrath is poured out in judgment upon the earth. Jesus Christ is our ark, and He will save us from the awesome judgment of God upon the earth.

God is not going to tolerate this madness and evil much longer. It is true that God is a God of love: John 3:15–17 says

> that whoever believes in Him should not perish but have eternal life. For God so loved the world that He gave His only begotten Son, that whoever believes in Him should not perish but have everlasting life. For God did not send His Son into the world to condemn the world, but that the world through Him might be saved.

God is not some cosmic cop up in the sky shouting to the human race "you're busted!" He loves mankind and each one of us so much that He sent His Son to die for our sins. Yet, because He is a God of love, He is going to put an end to all the suffering, hurt, pain, violence, and evil on planet earth.

God cannot continue to sit idly by and watch little children be sexually molested; He cannot tolerate women being raped, murders, war, brutality, disease, famine, and destruction. He is being patient so that every person has an opportunity to receive Jesus Christ and inherit God's free gift of salvation. But, at a moment only known to Him, He is going to swiftly put an end to all the evil on planet earth, and there will be a day of judgment.

Today people have become spiritually blind. They seem to think they can do anything and get away with it. But, as that popular song sung by Bette Midler says, "God is watching us from the distance." However, God may be watching us from the distance, but He can see us close-up. Nothing we do is hidden from God.

Perilous Times

In 2 Timothy 3:1–5 the Apostle Paul writes,

> But know this, in the last days perilous times will come: For men will be lovers of themselves, lovers of money, boasters, proud, blasphemers, disobedient to parents, unthankful, unholy, unloving, unforgiving, slanderers without self-control, brutal despisers of good, traitors, headstrong, haughty, lovers of pleasure rather than lovers of God. Having a form of godliness but denying its power. And from such people turn away.

This passage of Scripture sounds as if the Apostle Paul was describing our world today. Can you imagine the Apostle Paul coming back to our time today and picking up a remote control and channel surfing through your local cable system and watching MTV, "Geraldo," "Donahue," "Melrose Place," "Beverly Hills 90210," "A

Current Affair," "Hard Copy," and so on? I think the Apostle Paul would want to get raptured real quick.

In Matthew 24:12 Jesus said concerning the last days, "And because lawlessness will abound, the love of many will grow cold." In other words, Jesus is saying that society will be cold-hearted in the days which immediately precede His return. Just look at what modern society has become: a mother murders her two children; O.J. Simpson is accused of brutally murdering his wife, Nicole Simpson; a person gets mad at another driver on the freeway and blows them away with a gun; the Menendez brothers are brought to trial for murdering their parents; Tonya Harding is accused of "dirty tricks" in order to win a gold medal in ice skating; a wife cuts off her husband's penis and throws it out of a car window. It all sounds like madness, but it has become the regular fare of the tabloids and evening news.

Just consider the recent statistics regarding our culture as evidence of the breakdown of our society: Married couples now make up only 26 percent of the U.S. households, which is down 40 percent since 1970. This means that the other people are living together, sleeping around, divorced, or single. A little child will have watched eight thousand murders on television and over one hundred thousand acts of senseless violence before finishing elementary school. The number of child abuse victims has skyrocketed 40 percent between 1985 and 1991. Over 26 percent of girls age fifteen claim to be sexually active as compared to only 5 percent in 1970. Children under seventeen years old are 244 percent more likely to be killed by handguns than they were just a decade ago (Jerry Adler, "Kids Growing Up Scared," *Newsweek* [10 January 1994]: 44).

But, these statistics are just the tip of the iceberg. According to the National Academy of Sciences, nearly one-third of every crime involves violence, and, out of every one thousand crimes, three hundred involve serious aggravated assault with weapons. Although, crime is up across the globe, the National Academy of Sciences stated that the murder rate in the United States is higher than any other industrialized nation. In addition, the United States leads other nations in the incidence of serious and violent sexual assaults.

The FBI, the Office of Justice Programs, and the U.S. Department of Justice released statistics that revealed that during a sample year in the United States there were 18.8 million victimizations involving violence or personal theft. In addition, 14.8 million household crimes were committed. That's over 33 million violent crimes of rape, robbery, aggravated and simple assault, personal thefts, and household crimes of burglary, larceny, and car theft per year.

There are over one hundred thousand sex offenders in our jails serving time for rape, child molestation, and other crimes. However, the vast majority of sex offenders are not in jail but are out in society. In Washington State, a man named Earl Shriner abducted a seven-year-old boy, raped him, and castrated him. However, the boy lived and identified Shriner who was out of jail even though authorities knew he was dangerous. In Hamiltown, New Jersey, convicted pedophile Jesse Timmendequas was released by authorities to move into a middle class neighborhood with children. The authorities never bothered to notify the community of who had moved in among them. A seven-year-old girl was lured into the house of Timmendequas, who raped and strangled the little girl.

According to Bureau of Justice statistics nearly 8 percent of all rapists who are arrested rape again within three years of being released. Other studies show that 35 percent of all rapists will rape again after being released from jail. The statistics on pedophiles, exhibitionists, and other sexual deviants show similar trends of committing the same crimes they were arrested for soon after being released from jail.

Pedophiles are now using computer bulletin board systems (BBS) to lure young victims into sexual encounters. A fifty-one-year-old insurance salesman pretended to be a thirteen-year-old boy on computer E-mail. The insurance salesman thought he was luring a young boy named "Marty." However, "Marty" turned out to be a high-tech crimes detective from the San Jose Police Department, and the insurance salesman was busted: the police found in his car all kinds of sexual devices and pornography.

The words of Jesus Christ ring true in our day when He warned that lawlessness will abound and the love of many will grow cold. We live in a sick, twisted, and violent society, and it is not only happening in the United States but around the globe. The Bible teaches us that God does not allow this kind of wickedness to continue unchecked. In Matthew 24:37–39, Jesus Christ compares the last days to the days of Noah when He said, "But as the days of Noah were, so also will be the coming of the Son of Man be. For as in the days before the flood, they were eating and drinking, marrying and giving in marriage, until the day that Noah entered the ark, and did not know until the flood came and took them all away, so also will the coming of the Son of Man be." In this passage of Scripture, Jesus tells us that the sinful people of Noah's time were so caught up in partying, marriage, and living that they ignored Noah's warning and the reality of a soon coming flood. They were caught completely off-guard when the flood came, and Noah was supernaturally rescued by God.

However, if we go back to the Book of Genesis and the account of Noah, we learn some very interesting things. During the time of Noah, mankind had become very violent and perverted like today. In Genesis 6:5 we read, "Then the Lord saw that the wickedness of man was great in the earth, and that every intent of the thoughts of his heart was evil continually." Genesis 6:11 says, "The earth was also corrupt before God, and the earth was filled with violence." Our time is very much like Noah's time in that our world has become filled with violence, and society has become corrupt. It is a sign of the times that men's hearts have grown cold, and lawlessness has increased. Just as in Noah's time, there will come a time when God will put an end to all the wickedness and violence, and I believe that we are rapidly approaching that moment in history.

The Coming Apocalypse

According to the Worldwatch Institute's 1995 State of the World report, there is a bleak future ahead for mankind. Dwindling food supplies, environmental problems, and population problems threaten mankind's future. According to Worldwatch, rising population, overharvesting of fish, depletion of forests, and the abuse of groundwater reserves will create global unemployment, inflation, and economic hardship in many nations ("Institute Says Earth's Losses Put Us All on Shaky Ground," *Los Angeles Times*, 23 January 1995).

In order to manage the crisis, Worldwatch wants to strengthen the power of the United Nations and calls for governments to adhere to a 1994 World Population Plan of Action written at the United Nations conference in Cairo, Egypt, which sets a world population goal of 9.8 billion people by the year 2050. Critics of these projections claim that the earth can easily feed over 10 billion people with technology and free trade.

However, residents in Goma, Zaire, believed they were living in the beginning of the final days of the apocalypse in response to a mass exodus of Rwanda where millions have fled war, starvation, and disease. Some experts believe that half the country's population of 7.5 million people could potentially die. Across the planet there is an increase of famines, disease, and war that is nothing short of apocalyptic.

By the year 2050 there will be an estimated population of 9.5 billion people; by the year 2100 there would be 12 billion people alive on planet earth. However, political upheavals like the civil war in Rwanda between the Hutu and Tutsi tribes threaten the ability to feed people.

Although organizations like Zero Population Growth and the Pew Global Stewardship Initiative call for contraception and abortion as solutions to the problem, it appears the real problem is the slowdown in worldwide food production and political problems that block effective food distribution: Reportedly, grain is in surplus, and 46 million acres of U.S. farmland and 11 million acres in Europe have been deliberately been made barren by government programs ("10 Billion for Dinner Please," *U.S. News & World Report* [12 September 1994]).

Pestilences, Plagues, and Diseases

In Matthew 24:7, Jesus Christ warned that at the end of the age there would be various signs to alert us. Jesus said, "For nation will rise against nation, and kingdom against kingdom. And there will be famines, pestilences, and earthquakes in various places." The word pestilence comes from the Greek word *loimos*, which means plague or disease. Jesus Christ was warning us that in the time before His return there would be outbreaks of diseases and plagues.

A little over a decade ago modern medicine thought that they had conquered the majority of deadly diseases with the use of antibiotics and other medicines. However, recently, there has arisen a whole new generation of diseases which have become immune to antibiotics and for which we have no known cure. In Los Angeles recently, a man died of a new rare flesh-eating bacteria. He thought he had a sore throat and then he died the next day. These strange diseases may seem like something out of a science fiction movie until you know someone who catches one. A friend of ours was very close to the man who died, and it was a horrible thing. In Zaire, Africa, hundreds of people died from an outbreak of the Ebola virus and in Minnesota a killer bug of meningitis spread throughout a small town.

In her book *The Coming Plague—Newly Emerging Diseases in a World out of Balance* (Farrar, Straus and Giroux,

1994), Laurie Garrett, warns of new plagues of AIDS, malaria, lyme disease, the Marbug virus, Legionnaires disease, the Hanta virus, new forms of syphilis and gonorrhea, cholera, etc. According to Garett (who was a former science correspondent for National Public Radio and now a science writer for *Newsday*), sex, drugs, war, and travel are helping to spread diseases rapidly worldwide.

Garrett relates that during the mid-twentieth century many scientists and policy-makers believed that vaccines and antibiotics would prevent infectious diseases. But, historic diseases like TB, measles, cholera, and syphilis are making a deadly comeback. Due to sexual promiscuity and heterosexual and homosexual prostitution, sexually transmitted diseases have increased, while war and civil strife in places like Rwanda have caused outbreaks of cholera.

According to her research over 21 million people were living as refugees or in war zones in 1993, which helped to spread disease through contaminated food, poor sanitation, close living quarters, and sexual promiscuity (Fitzhugh Mullan, "The Silent Killers," *Los Angeles Times*, 6 November 1994, 3). The World Health Organization (WHO) predicts that there will be over 40 million cases of HIV by the year 2000. According to WHO research, in 1993 there were 1 million HIV cases in North America; 500,000 in Western Europe; 50,000 in Eastern Europe and Central Asia; 1.5 million in Latin America and the Caribbean; over 8 million in the Sub-Sahara region of Africa; 25,000 in East Asia and the Pacific; 1.5 million in South and Southeast Asia, and 25,000 in Australia (Connie Zhu, "Global AIDS Epidemic Looms," *Christian American* [Feb. 1994]: 6).

Dr. James Chin, an epidemiologist in charge of AID's research at the World Health Organization, believes that by the year 2000 heterosexuals will be the primary carriers of AIDS in industrial nations, with a breakdown of 70 percent heterosexual, 10 percent homosexual, and 10 percent due to drug users who use needles. AIDS has now

passed cancer, heart disease, and accidents as the leading
cause of death among men twenty-five to forty-four years
of age in California. In New York, New Jersey, Florida,
and Massachusetts, AIDS and its related diseases are the
leading killers of young men (ibid., 6).

A growing danger among monogamous and nondrug-
abusing heterosexuals is the increased risk of secondary
infections such as new drug-resistant strains of tuberculosis, which can be carried through the air, or the risk to
young children who are mysteriously catching the disease. Many individuals who are HIV positive are carriers
of drug-resistant strains of TB. As such, there is a TB
epidemic in the United States, which is directly related to
the HIV virus.

Interestingly, Jesus Christ warned of an increase in
plagues and pestilences in the last days centuries before
AIDS was ever around. Many of these new diseases and
plagues are related to mankind's sinful behavior such as
war, drug use, and sexual promiscuity.

There have been some who even have suggested that
some of the new diseases that we have been seeing have
come out of biological warfare laboratories. There are
some scientists and doctors who have proposed that the
AIDS virus, the Hanta virus, Legionnaires disease, and
many of the new designer viruses were developed in biological warfare laboratories.

Doomsday Cults

Jesus Christ said, "For false christs and false prophets
will rise" (Matt. 24:24). In recent years we have seen an
increase in these false christs. In Tokyo, Japan, the cult
Aum Supreme Truth's leader Shoko Asahara, who claims
to be the Messiah, is being investigated by the police for
a chemical warfare attack on a Japanese subway which
killed ten people and injured five thousand more. This
strange cult, which has bizarre rituals like drinking their
guru's blood in order to ingest his DNA and wearing
helmets equipped with electrodes designed to stimulate

the brain, is just one of over two hundred thousand different religious groups that have grown up out of Japan in this century. Ironically, this cult was called the Science of Happiness.

There seems to be an increase of doomsday-style cults. Consider David Koresh of the Branch Davidians in Waco, Texas. In Switzerland, Luc Jouret a forty-six-year-old homeopathic physician led a cult where twenty-five burned bodies were found in the Alpine village of Granges-sur-Salvan, and no one can forget the horrible mass suicide led by Jim Jones in Jonestown, Guyana.

The only explanation for this is a rise in demonic activity where charismatic leaders, who are energized by what I believe are supernatural forces, seduce people to their death. There is something inherent in the nature of evil which seeks to bring people to their destruction. What we are seeing on a global level is false christs empowered by Satan who are attempting to destroy people.

The Oklahoma Tragedy

No one can forget the horrifying scenes of a federal building in Oklahoma blown apart by a powerful bomb. Over two hundred people, some of them small children, were murdered by madmen who launched a personal vendetta against the U.S. government. These are truly times where, in the words of Jesus Christ, "lawlessness has increased" and "men's hearts have grown cold." To think that Americans would deliberately murder fellow Americans and innocent children would have been unthinkable just a generation ago.

Instead of using the political process in an attempt to change the system, these homegrown terrorists allowed the seeds of hatred, bitterness, and murder to grow in their hearts. Then, in a sociopathic and murderous rage they slaughtered the innocent in cold blood. No amount of antigovernment rhetoric can justify the act, for it plainly was an evil, wicked, and cruel act of hideous violence.

Terror 101

The cult Aum Supreme Truth in Japan and the bombing of the Oklahoma City federal building woke the world
up to the dangers of terrorism in our society. Although
nuclear weapons possess the greatest threat of all, biological weapons of mass destruction can be silent but
deadly. Robert Wright writing for the magazine *The New
Republic* states, "A small, private airplane with 220 pounds
of anthrax spores could fly over Washington on a north
south route . . . and trail an invisible mist that would kill
a million people on a day with a moderate wind" (Robert
Wright, "Be Very Afraid—Nukes, Nerve Gas and Anthrax
spores—Washington D.C.," *The New Republic* [1 May 1995]:
23, 26).

Wright says that the danger of a potent virus like
anthrax is that it takes a couple of days before it starts to
kill people, and the terrorist could be vacationing in the
Caribbean before anyone figured out what happened. The
possible scenarios involving biological warfare are endless. Kyle Olson of the Chemical and Biological Warfare
Institute says that a New York City taxi cab could be
equipped with an aerosol-type sprayer in its trunk that
could spray out a fine mist of anthrax as it was driving
around New York City. In a couple of days tens of thousands of people would be mysteriously dying all over the
city (ibid.).

Yet, anthrax is still an older generation of a biological
warfare virus. New designer viruses are being concocted
in secret laboratories around the world. In fact, these new
designer viruses could be created to attack certain ethnic,
gender, or racial groups that have certain predisposed
genetic weaknesses (ibid.). The whole thing is completely
bone-chilling.

The lesson of Oklahoma City and of the Aum Supreme Truth cult is that there are groups and individuals
who are ready to use these weapons should they be able
to get their hands on them. Can you imagine a terrorist

group holding the United States hostage with the threat of a nuclear or biological weapon in one of our major U.S. cities?

Nations like Saddam Hussein's Iraq are already thought to be involved in the clandestine manufacturing of nuclear and biological weapons. North Korea and Communist China are also manufacturing chemical, biological, and nuclear weapons of mass destruction. One of the scenarios of using biological weapons is to give the user of the weapon a special vaccine so that his nation remains immune to the destruction that the virus will release.

If the madmen in Oklahoma City or the cult in Japan had their hands on nuclear or biological weapons like anthrax they would have used it. The death toll would have been hundreds or thousands of times greater. Perhaps when Jesus Christ talked about the increase of "pestilences" in the last days, He knew full well of mankind's intent to manufacture biological weapons.

Chapter Four

Then Shall the End Come

In Matthew 24:3 Jesus Christ's disciples asked Him when the end would come: "Now as He sat on the Mount of Olives, the disciples came to Him privately, saying 'Tell us, when will be the sign of Your coming, and of the end of the age?' " Jesus Christ went on to list an entire series of circumstances that would occur before the end of the age. But, perhaps the most significant occurrence that Jesus spoke of was in Matthew 24:14 when He said, "And this gospel of the kingdom will be preached in all the world as a witness to all nations, and then the end shall come."

The greatest sign of all is that the gospel of the kingdom will be preached throughout all the earth, and this is precisely what is happening in our day in an unprecedented manner. In fact, 70 percent of all world evangelism has taken place since the year 1900, and 70 percent of that progress has happened since World War II. It is interesting to note that the greatest explosion of world evangelism has happened since the time that Israel became a nation again in 1948.

All across the globe, millions are accepting Jesus Christ as their Lord and Savior as never before. Since the fall of communism in Russia, over thirty million people have come to Christ. In Communist China, over seventy-five million out of the one billion population have received Jesus into their lives. In Latin America, there were only fifty thousand "born-again" believers in 1900. By 1980

that figure had climbed to twenty million, and by the year
A.D. 2000 there will be over one hundred million "born-
again" believers in Latin America (*Signs of the Times,* CBN
video, 1994). Research suggests that across the planet,
Christianity is growing three times faster than the world's
population.

Some believe that we are experiencing the final thrust
of world evangelism in the 1990s. For over two thousand
years the truth of the gospel of Jesus Christ has spread
across the world, and it is believed by many that Satan is
now backed up into his last stronghold, which is called
the "10/40 window." The 10/40 window is a large geographic region stretching from West Africa to Japan. It is
where 97 percent of the world's unevangelized live and
consists of over sixty-two nations.

There are over four billion people who live in the 10/
40 window, and it is the world's headquarters of religions
like Islam, Buddhism, and Shintoism. It is the global center of Eastern mysticism, ancestor worship, and Islamic
fundamentalism. But, prayer experts like Dick Eastman
of "Praying Through the 10/40 Window" believe that the
walls are tumbling down and that mass evangelism will
soon occur in these areas. (Source for the above is *Signs
of the Times* video from CBN [1994]).

In addition, millions of people from nations like India, Pakistan, Iran, China, Vietnam, Japan, West Africa,
and other nations are moving to places like Los Angeles
where they are being exposed to the gospel for the first
time in their lives and are then bringing the truth of
Jesus to their homelands. Evangelists like Dr. Christopher Sun have held massive crusades in Los Angeles and
Malaysia, where Sun has preached in both Chinese and
English.

Evangelists like Billy Graham preached to over one
billion people in over 175 countries via satellite during
an event called Global Mission. The crusade was broadcast live from San Juan, Puerto Rico, to eight million

people attending satellite crusades in 2,200 countries and translated in over one hundred languages. In addition, an audience of over one billion people will watch the crusade through prime-time broadcasts on national television networks in over one hundred nations.

Earthquake-rocked Kobe, Japan, was one of the mission sites along with Goma, Zaire, where more than 1.8 million Rwandan refugees still live. Never before in the history of mankind have over one billion people heard the message of the gospel in such a short period of time. Clearly, we are seeing the fulfillment of Matthew 24:14 where the gospel of the kingdom is being preached throughout the earth.

The Ten Nation Kingdom: Sign of the End

One of the major biblical signs that we are in the last days is the prediction that there will be a ten nation revival of the Roman Empire. Although the Bible does not name these ten countries, many Bible scholars believe that they might include Italy and Germany along with major countries in southern Europe and maybe some nations in western Asia and northern Africa.

The Bible speaks of a political union of the ten nations and then of a dictator emerging called the Antichrist. The Anti-christ will expand his ten nation confederacy into a one-world government (Rev. 17:12-13). In these verses, the ten horns represent the ten nations, or ten kings, that will rule during this time. This prophecy has never been fulfilled because there has never been a time in the Roman Empire when ten kings have ruled. However, with the emergence of something like the United States of Europe, this will be possible. In addition, although a nation like Germany attempted twice to conquer the world and establish a world government during World War I and II, this plan has never yet been successful.

The coming of a one-world government is one of the signs that we are living in the general time period that will precede the Second Coming of Jesus Christ.

The Beast Factor

Imagine a world run by an evil genius with total dictatorial control. The Bible talks about such a world with a coming global ruler called the Anti-christ or the Beast. Revelation 13:1–7 says:

> Then I stood on the sand of the sea. And I saw a beast rising up out of the sea, having seven heads and ten horns, and on his horns ten crowns, and on his heads a blasphemous name.
>
> Now the beast which I saw was like a leopard, and his feet were like the feet of a bear, and his mouth like the mouth of a lion. The dragon gave him his power, his throne, and great authority.
>
> And I saw one of his heads as if it had been mortally wounded, and his deadly wound was healed. And all the world marveled and followed the beast.
>
> So they worshiped the dragon who gave authority to the beast; and they worshipped the beast saying, "Who is like the beast? Who is able to make war with him?"
>
> And he was given a mouth speaking great things and blasphemies, and he was given authority to continue for forty-two months.
>
> Then he opened his mouth in blasphemy against God, to blaspheme His name, His tabernacle, and those who dwell in heaven.
>
> It was granted to him to make war with the saints and to overcome them. And authority was given him over every tribe, tongue and nation.
>
> All who dwell on the earth will worship him, whose names have not been written in the Book of Life of the Lamb slain from the foundation of the world.

Here the Bible predicts that a future leader (the Beast) is going to rise up from ten horns of some kind of political power, which some believe will be a ten nation European confederacy. This charismatic leader is going to be worshiped just like God, and he will oppose God's people who are on the earth at that time (Rev. 13:8). It's not hard to imagine that with the new technology such as the "information superhighway," a seductive political leader will be able to communicate with and control the whole earth.

The Beast Rising Up Out of the Sea

> Then I stood on the sand of the sea. And I saw a beast rising up out of the sea, having seven heads and ten horns, and on his horns ten crowns, and on his heads a blasphemous name. Now the beast which I saw was like a leopard, his feet were like the feet of a bear, and his mouth like the mouth of a lion. The dragon gave him his power, his throne and great authority.

This passage of Scripture in Revelation is directly tied to the vision of the four beasts that Daniel had in Daniel 7:2–7.

Late in the sixth century B.C., the prophet Daniel, who was deported as a teen-ager in 605 B.C. to Babylon where he served as a trainee in Nebuchadnezzar's court and later served as an advisor to foreign kings, had a powerful vision of the end times. Daniel 7:2–7 states,

> Daniel spoke, saying, "I saw in my vision by night, and behold, the four winds of heaven were stirring up the great sea. And four beasts came up from the sea, each different from the other. The first was like a lion, and had eagles wings. I watched till its wings were plucked off; and was lifted up from the earth and made to stand on two feet like a man, and a man's heart was given to it. And suddenly another beast, a second like a bear. It was raised up on one side, and had three ribs in its mouth between its teeth. And they said thus to it: 'Arise devour much flesh!' After this I looked, and there

was another, like a leopard, which had on its back four wings of a bird. The beast also had four heads, and dominion was given to it. After this I saw in the night visions, and behold a fourth beast, dreadful and terrible, exceedingly strong. It had huge iron teeth; it was devouring, breaking in pieces, and trampling the residue with its feet. It was different from all the beasts that were before it and it had ten horns."

Many Bible scholars agree that the beasts represent various kingdoms that will arise in succession. The lion represents the Babylonian Empire, the bear portrays the Media or Medo-Persian Empire, and the leopard represents the Greek Empire. The fourth beast represents the Roman Empire with a future ten nation confederacy. The Roman Empire consists of two phases. Phase one is the Roman Empire that seized power around 68 B.C. and then disappeared. In Phase two of the Roman Empire there will be some kind of ten nation confederacy led by the Anti-christ.

The European Economic Community consists of twelve members, and it is growing. Currently the twelve nations are Belgium, Denmark, France, Germany, Greece, England, Ireland, Italy, Luxembourg, the Netherlands, Portugal, and Spain. In addition, Finland, Norway, Austria, Iceland, Switzerland, Liechtenstein, Hungry, and Czechoslovakia are either seeking membership or increased representation in the EEC.

With the ratification of the Maastricht Treaty, Europe is moving ever closer towards becoming a unified entity. On 1 January 1994 the European Monetary Institute was created; in 1997 a European Central Bank will start operation and will have the power to set rates for exchanging the different currencies into a new single European currency; and on 1 January 1999 the single new European currency, or EC, will be issued.

Obviously, in order for the United Europe to become the fourth beast prophesied by Daniel as having ten horns, a number of different things will have to happen. Either the membership of the European Economic Community will have to become smaller, with some nations dropping out, or there will have to be a consolidation of nations. However, another scenario is also a possibility. Some Bible prophecy experts have suggested that perhaps this concept of a ten nation confederacy needs to be expanded to some kind of ten global regions in a one-world government. In other words, the ten horns of the revived Roman Empire could be some kind of one-world government consisting of ten regions such as North and South America, Africa, Europe, etc.

In any case, there is a time coming when a powerful charismatic leader whom the Bible calls the Anti-christ will assume control of some kind of global government and rule the world for a limited period of time.

The Fourth Kingdom

In Daniel, chapter 7, we read about Daniel's vision of the four beasts: "After this I saw in a night vision, and behold a fourth beast, dreadful and terrible, exceedingly strong. It had huge iron teeth; it was devouring, breaking in pieces, and trampling the residue with its feet. It was different from all the beasts that were before it, and it had ten horns" (Dan. 7:7).

A little later on Daniel writes, "The fourth beast shall be a fourth kingdom on earth, which shall be different from all other kingdoms, and shall devour the whole earth, trample it and break it in pieces. The ten horns are ten kings who shall rise from this kingdom" (Dan. 7:23–24). Here we read about the revival of the Roman Empire. However, unlike the Roman Empire, this kingdom "shall be different than all kingdoms" (Dan. 7:23).

In Revelation 17:12–14, John writes,

> The ten horns which you saw are ten kings who have received no kingdom as yet, but they receive authority for one hour as kings with the beast. These are of one mind, and they will give power and

authority to the beast. These will make war with the
Lamb, and the Lamb will overcome them, for He
is Lord of lords and King of kings; and those who
are with Him are called chosen, and faithful.

In these verses, the Bible is speaking of some kind of
one-world government that comes from a revived Roman
Empire and may consist of either ten European nations
or ten regions dividing up planet earth. Jacques Delors,
who is one of the major leaders in building the new Europe and the European Economic Community, describes
the new Europe as similar to Greece, Rome, and
Christendom. He talks about a United Europe that will
incorporate the best traditions of "Roman law, the Greek
spirit, and the personality of Christianity" (Daniel Burstein,
*Euroquake—Europe's Explosive Economic Challenge Will
Change the World* [New York: Simon & Schuster, 1991],
59).

Daniel Burstein writes in his book *Euroquake—Europe's
Explosive Economic Challenge Will Change the World,*

> The idea of a unified Europe is anything but new.
> Two thousand years ago, the Romans presided over
> a "common European economic space" that would
> make today's Eurocrats envious. Roman coins func-
> tioned as common currency. Common "technical
> standards"—such as the Roman alphabet, numeri-
> cal system, measurements and architectural prin-
> ciples—were accepted almost everywhere in the
> empire. . . . Roman leaders even enjoyed what
> today's European unifiers do not dare discuss: a
> common language. [p. 126]

Beginning in 1992 Europe has been on the fast track
in uniting this revived Roman Empire with the advent of
the European Economic Community. By the end of 1993,
the EEC was the largest single market in the world, and
in 1997 the EC will become the common currency for the
European Economic Community backed by the EuroFed
central banking system. Finally, by the year 2000 the EEC

will become the United States of Europe with its own president.

What the American media and politicians have been slow to tell the American people is that this rise of the European Economic Community signals the end of America as the world's leading superpower. Is it possible that this United States of Europe is the ten nation confederacy spoken of by the prophet Daniel in Daniel, chapter 7? Is this the political state described in Revelation, chapter 13, which the Beast or Anti-christ emerges to lead?

The Tower of Babel

Many times modern man makes the mistake in thinking that civilizations before our time were primitive and backwards. In Genesis 11 we read about the Chaldaic nation which built the Tower of Babel. This geographic region became what is known as Babylon. The Chaldeans were a very advanced people that had many similarities to our world today. Historians and archeologists have discovered information that suggests that the Chaldeans had discovered the principles of aerodynamics and had constructed the first wind-powered airplane. In addition, there is evidence to suggest that they were sophisticated enough to practice advanced medical techniques such as difficult brain surgery.

Ancient Babylon was the spiritual fountainhead for all the occult religions that exist today. Nimrod was the ruler of Babylon, and in Genesis 10:9 the Bible calls him "a mighty hunter." However, Nimrod was not just a hunter of animals, but of the souls of men, and he was used by Satan to deceive mankind. Nimrod defied God and built the Tower of Babel, which was an attempt to reach heaven through occult means. Further, all the astrological and zodiac religions can be traced back to ancient Babylon and Nimrod.

Nimrod's wife, Semiramis, was called the Supreme One, or the priestess. This was the beginning of the mystery religion of Babylon. Semiramis came to be called

Queen of Heaven, and she was worshiped as a god. This pagan belief soon swept throughout the ancient world. In Egypt she was called Isis, in Asia Cybele, in Greece Aphrodite, and in Rome Venus. Today, there is a great movement to reestablish the goddess religions and all of the goddesses flow out of ancient Babylonian occult beliefs.

The Tower of Babel and One-World Government

The concept of a one-world government flows out of the occult belief system that built the Tower of Babel. During this time in history, mankind had "one language" and "one speech" (Gen. 11:11). This is why modern linguists believe that mankind had an original common language. The people of the whole earth were united as one through a common language, and they attempted to exalt themselves as gods and control the planet.

God did not take lightly their attempt to reach heaven through self-exaltation. Genesis 11:6–9 states,

> And the Lord said, "Indeed the people are one and they all have one language, and this is what they begin to do; now nothing that they propose to do will be withheld from them. Come, let Us go down and there confuse their language, that they may not understand one another's speech." So the Lord scattered them abroad from over the face of the earth, and they ceased building the city. Therefore its name is called Babel, because the Lord confused the language of the whole earth; and from there the Lord scattered them abroad over the face the earth.

The word *Babel* comes from the Hebrew word *balal*, which means "mixed up" or "confused." Later on the Babylonians came to interpret *Babel* as "the gate of God." The Tower of Babel was the origin of the ancient city of Babylon. It represents the world system which attempts to take the place of God. This is exactly what modern humanism has done. It tells mankind that every man is a god and places the government in the place of God.

In the Book of Revelation we read about a one-world government where the Anti-christ will rule the world. Revelation 13:7 states, "It was granted to him [the Beast] to make war with the saints and to overcome them. And authority was given to him over every tribe, tongue and nation." Revelation 17:1–5 states,

> Then one of the seven angels who had seven bowls came and talked with me, saying to me, "Come I will show you the judgment of the great harlot who sits on many waters, with whom the kings of the earth committed fornication, and the inhabitants of the earth were made drunk with the wine of her fornication." So he carried me away in the Spirit into the wilderness. And I saw a woman sitting on a scarlet beast which was full of names of blasphemy, having seven heads and ten horns. The woman was arrayed in purple and scarlet, and adorned with gold and precious stones and pearls, having in her hand a golden cup full of abominations and the filthiness of her fornication. And on her forehead a name was written: Mystery, Babylon the Great the Mother of Harlots and the Abominations of the Earth.

In the last days, the Anti-christ will rule over Babylon, which has its roots in the ancient Tower of Babel built by Nimrod, who was a type of the Anti-christ. In ancient Rome, prostitutes were ordered to wear a label on their foreheads with their name written on it so that everyone would know they were prostitutes. In Revelation 17:12–13, 17–18, we read about this coming one-world government, which will be ruled by the Anti-christ and which will be an expression of the Babylonian world system, which is the great whore because it exists in opposition to God.

> The ten horns which you saw are ten kings who have received no kingdom as yet, but they receive

authority for one hour as kings with the beast. These are of one mind, and they will give their power and authority to the beast. . . . For God will put it into their hearts to fulfill His purpose, to be of one mind, and to give their kingdom to the beast, until the words of God are fulfilled. And the woman you saw is that great city which reigns over the kings of the earth.

This passage of Scripture is very similar to Genesis 11:6 where the Bible declares, "And the Lord said, 'Indeed the people are one and they all have a one language, and this is what they begin to do; now nothing will be withheld from them.' " The current movement towards a new world order goes all the way back to the Tower of Babel. The new world order will be judged by God just like in the days of the Tower of Babel.

A Ten Nation Confederacy

As we have discussed earlier, there is a global push towards some kind of new one-world order. The European Economic Community has just passed a $37 billion recovery plan to involve Britain and Denmark in economic incentives to develop a closer union provided by the Maastricht Treaty. The European Parliament now has 567 seats, and the European Economic Community is expected to grow from twelve nations to over twenty.

Although Daniel, chapters 2 and 7, talks about a ten nation confederacy revived out of the old Roman Empire, continued political changes in the European Economic Community could well bring this about. In Daniel, 2:31–45, four successive kingdoms are discussed. The Babylonian, Medo-Persian, Grecian, and possibly the revived Roman Empire. And, in Daniel 7:1–8 we see Daniel talking about the various kingdoms represented by different beasts. The lion represents Babylon; the bear represents either Media or the Medo-Persian Empire; and the leopard represents either Persia or Greece. The fourth beast could possibly represent a revived Roman Empire and some kind of ten nation European confederacy.

Chapter Five

Rebuilding the Temple

D aniel 9:27 explains how the Anti-christ will end the sacrifices in the temple and set himself up to be worshipped. "Then he [the Anti-christ] shall confirm a covenant with many for one week; But in the middle of the week he shall bring an end to sacrifice and offering. And on the wing of abominations shall be one who makes desolate, even until the consummation, which is determined, is poured out on the desolate."

Although some people confine this prophecy to the time of Antiochus Epiphanes in the second century who set up a heathen altar in the temple, many people, including this author, believe that it is pointing to a future time when a last days Anti-christ will desecrate the temple. In Revelation 11:1–2 we see a time when the Jewish temple along with its system of worship is restored. A number of Bible scholars believe that this temple will be restored in the first three and one half years of the Great Tribulation, or Daniel's Seventieth Week (Dan. 9:24–27).

This event will be followed by "the abomination of desolation," where the Anti-christ will put an end to sacrifices in the rebuilt temple and demand that people worship him instead of God. This will be the final fulfillment of the ultimate evil in mankind's fall. Men and women will choose to worship Satan instead of God. It will be the consummation of all humanistic, occultic, and New Age ideas. It will be the ultimate deception of the human race (Dan. 11:31-36).

However, in order for this event to occur, the ancient Jewish temple must first be rebuilt. Right now in Israel there is a powerful movement of people who are actively making plans to rebuild the temple. In fact, every sacrificial instrument has been especially recreated in accordance with the strictest of Hebrew regulations so that the animal sacrifices can once again be carried on in the temple. Not only have the Orthodox Jews created a special computer database with over twenty-eight thousand men who have the genealogical background to be in the priesthood, they have even dedicated the actual cornerstone of this temple.

According to Thomas Ice and Randall Price, who authored the book *Ready To Rebuild—The Imminent Plan To Rebuild the Last Days Temple*, there are several related groups in Jerusalem who are preparing for priestly service in the restored temple. Every year Jerusalem sees entire new industries that are active in promoting this idea of a third temple era. Two businesses are Beged Ivri, which literally means "Hebrew Clothing," founded by a thirty-two-year-old Orthodox Jew from Miami, Florida, who is manufacturing special levitical temple garments and Harrari Harps, which is making special biblical harps that were used during the time of the first and second temples. After more than two thousand years, these harps are again being built to play special music in the rebuilt temple (Thomas Ice and Randall Price, *Ready To Rebuild—The Imminent Plan To Rebuild the Last Days Temple* [Eugene, Oregon: Harvest House Publishers, 1992], 111, 113).

The rebuilding of the temple has some imminent and respected supporters. At the First Annual Temple Conference in Jerusalem, which was put on to discuss the plans for the third temple, a group of respected scientists gathered, including Dr. Gerald Schroeder, who wrote *Genesis and The Big Bang*; Dr. Asher Kaufman, who has suggested that the temple actually was to the north of the Dome of the Rock; Dr. Dan Bahat, who is the chief archaeologist of Jerusalem; Lambert Dolphin; and Gershon Salomon of the Temple Mount Faithful, who has been a tireless promoter of the third temple. Due to his efforts in attempting to rebuild the temple, Gershon Salomon was identified by the *Jerusalem Post* as the number one person on the PLO hit list!

For all these people and the many who support them, the plan for a rebuilt temple is soon becoming a reality. The first temple was built by Solomon; the second temple was built by Herod; and now the Jews are attempting to build a third temple. However, the construction of this third temple faces a major obstacle: in A.D. 638, Islam invaded Jerusalem and seized the Temple Mount. The Muslims are militantly opposed to the idea of Israel rebuilding the temple. They realize that in order for Islam to capture Israel totally they must prevent this third temple from being constructed. The present Dome of the Rock, a Muslim temple built over what many believe to be the site of the Jewish temple, appears to be blocking the construction of the third temple. However, God is in the miracle working business, and there are ways this problem can be solved.

Islam has controlled the Temple Mount for over thirteen hundred years, and men like Gershon Salomon, whose namesake Solomon built the first temple, are committed to the rebuilding project. Salomon is head of the Temple Mount and Eretz Yisrael Faithful movement, or TMF. He is a vegetarian who was wounded in the 1958 Sinai Campaign and fought in the Six-Day War in 1967. He was also a paratrooper in the Six-Day War and was part of a special unit which made it through to the Temple Mount. When he entered the Dome of the Rock with the other soldiers, they had a powerful experience with God as they realized they were standing on holy ground. Salomon and the other soldiers started to weep, and it changed his life forever—his goal is to remove the Moslem presence from the Temple Mount (ibid., 120–121).

At the Second Annual Jerusalem Temple Conference, Gershon spoke on the subject of *Israel's Spiritual Awakening and the Messiah's Coming*. Salomon and the other activists involved in rebuilding the temple realize that this is a key activity in prophetic fulfillment.

Daniel's Seventy Weeks

Around 536 B.C. the prophet Daniel received a powerful vision of the future of Israel and of the last days. While praying and seeking God, God sent to Daniel the angel Gabriel who helped reveal to Daniel how the refining judgments of Israel would come to an end and how they would finally accept their Messiah. This prophecy along with Romans 11 clearly demonstrates that Israel is God's prophetic time clock.

When reading Daniel 9:20–27, it is important to understand that the Jewish year during biblical times consisted of 360 days and not 365 days. The Jewish year was lunar-solar and not the 365.25 solar year that modern nations live under. The weeks of years (490 years) are 360 day years. If we compare Revelation 11:2, 3; 12:6, 14; and 13:5 with Daniel 7:25 we see that the Bible is talking about 360 day years.

Daniel's weeks of years started in 445 B.C. when the Persian King Artaxerxes Longimanus commanded that Jerusalem be rebuilt. Daniel's Seventy Weeks prophetic timetable is divided as follows:

The Seventy Weeks of Daniel

Seven Sevens 7 Weeks 49 Years	King Artaxerxes' commandment to the arrival of Nehemiah and the covenant renewal celebration at Jerusalem. 445 to 396 B.C.
Sixty-two Sevens 62 Weeks of Years 434 Years	Sixty-two sevens starting from the dedication of the second temple to the crucifixion of the Lord Jesus Christ. Israel rejected Jesus Christ as their Messiah on Palm Sunday A.D. 32.

One Seven
70th Week
7 Years

This seven-year period which is yet unfulfilled is where national Israel will enter into a covenant with the future little horn, or Anti-christ, for seven years. In the middle of the week, or three-and-one-half years, the Antichrist will break the covenant, stop the blood sacrifices restored by Israel in the last days and set up his own image in the Jewish temple and demand to be worshiped.

There are other interpretations of this passage of Scripture such as the classical interpretation, which regards the 490 years as not a literal time period, but rather a lifetime of punishment seven times over. In this view of things, Israel's desolation will last for many centuries until it finally comes to an end. Also, the people who look at Daniel's Seventy Weeks from the classical viewpoint believe that this prophecy basically deals with the second century B.C. when Jerusalem was conquered by Antiochus Epiphanes who set up an image of himself in the temple. Antiochus ruled Syria from 175 B.C. to 164 B.C.

Antiochus Epiphanes had an image of his chief god Zeus Olympus (which was carved with a face that looked like Antiochus himself) carried into the Holy of Holies of the temple. Over eighty thousand Jews were slain during this period, which culminated in Antiochus's overthrow and the Maccabean uprising. This classical interpretation does not rule out the possibility that the prophecy also applies to the destruction of Jerusalem or a future lasts days Anti-christ. However, I believe that Daniel's Seventy Weeks has its ultimate interpretation in the coming of the future Anti-christ. It is my opinion that God is trying to prepare His people in the last days for the eventual rise of the Anti-christ.

Although this passage of Scripture has partial fulfillment in Antiochus Epiphanes' setting up his god Zeus Olympus (or Baal Shamen which means the "Lord of

Heaven," worshiped among the pagans and the Hellenistic Jews who saw this image as an expression of the God of Israel), the ultimate meaning of this passage is revealed at the time of the end. In Revelation 11:1–2 we see the time when Jewish temple worship will be restored in the first three-and-one-half years of the Great Tribulation, which is known as Daniel's Seventieth Week. After this comes the "abomination of desolation," or the time when the Anti-christ will demand that all sacrifices in the temple be stopped and that he be worshiped as God.

Revelation 11:2 states, "But leave out the court which is outside the temple, and do not measure it, for it has been given to the Gentiles. And they will tread the holy city underfoot for forty-two months." This started in 605 B.C. when Judah went into captivity under King Nebuchadnezzar and will not come to an end until the Second Coming of Jesus Christ.

Many people believe that this time period was completed during the Six-Day War of 1967 when the Jews miraculously recaptured the ancient city of Jerusalem. Some people believe that the forty-two months speaks of limited time rather than a specific time period. However, I think that God is quite specific in the Bible and does not throw around numbers casually. The Bible is a very precise system of numbers, dates, and events. The God who hung the stars in their precise orbits and created the intricacy of the DNA code is not playing with numbers. When the Bible says forty-two months, God is talking about a specific time period.

The Seven Year Covenant

In Daniel 9:24–27 we read about Israel's prophetic future and a time yet to come during the last seven years where Israel would enter into covenant with the Anti-christ. Daniel 9:27 shows us that the seven years that precede the Second Coming of Christ will start when Israel signs a covenant with the Anti-christ. According to Daniel, this peace covenant will be observed for three-

and-one-half years, and then in the middle of this seven-year period, the Anti-christ will break the covenant with Israel.

In the middle of this seven-year period the Anti-christ will break his covenant with Israel and set up an abomination that causes desolation in the temple. This abomination of desolation will be some kind of image of the Anti-christ that is to be worshiped by the people. Daniel 12:11–12 states, "And from the time that the daily sacrifice is taken away, and the abomination of desolation is set up, there shall be one thousand two hundred and ninety days. Blessed is he who waits, and comes to one thousand three hundred and thirty-five days." The 1,290 days correspond to the three-and-one-half years. What the above passage means is that a blessing will come upon those who reach the end of this time because Jesus Christ will have returned and those still living will enter the Millennial kingdom.

However, prior to the Second Coming of Jesus Christ and his Millennial reign will be a time of unprecedented distress upon the planet. Daniel 12:1 states, "And there will be a time of trouble such as never was since there was a nation, Even to that time your people shall be delivered." When the Anti-christ sets up the abomination of desolation in the temple and breaks his covenant with Israel, the last three-and-one-half years of the seven-year period begins. This seven-year period is called the time of Jacob's trouble.

The prophet Jeremiah, who was alive during the time of Babylonian captivity said,

> For thus says the Lord: "We have heard a voice of trembling, Of fear, and not of peace. Ask now, and see. Whether a man is ever in labor with a child? So why do I see every man with his hands on his loins like a woman in labor, and all faces turned pale? Alas! For that day is great, So that none is like it; And it is the time of Jacob's trouble, But, he shall be saved out of it." (Jer. 30:5–7)

The pretribulation viewpoint on the Rapture is that the Church of Jesus Christ will be raptured before the Anti-christ signs the covenant with Israel. In other words, the Church will not be here for the Tribulation, the abomination of desolation, and the Great Tribulation. According to John F. Walvoord, "Essential to the question of determining the time of the Rapture is discerning the changed role of the Holy Spirit after the Rapture and in between the period between the Rapture and the Second Coming. . . . Paul refutes the early posttribulationism that invaded the Thessalonian church with the argument that the events of the Day of the Lord were not taking place. Among them was his pointed reference to the revelation of the man of lawlessness, the political leader of the ten-nation group of the end-time as the final world ruler dominated by Satan. Paul's point is that he cannot be revealed until that which is restraining sin is removed" (John F. Walvoord, *Major Bible Prophecies—37 Crucial Prophecies That Affect You Today* [New York: Zondervan Publishing, a division of HarperCollins 1991], 334).

In 2 Thessalonians 2:1–12, the Apostle Paul talks about the revealing of the man of sin, or the Anti-christ. Although there has been great debate to exactly what the restraining force is that is holding back or restraining the Anti-christ, one of the more popular theories is that the restraining force is human government. But, many Pretribulationists such as Walvoord suggest that this is impossible because in the end times the entire government of the Anti-christ will be evil. Walvoord believes that the restraining force must be God himself and the presence of the Holy Spirit inside the lives of believers in Jesus Christ, who are the Church (ibid., 323).

Walvoord says that the only way that the Anti-christ can be revealed is when the restraining force is removed through the Rapture of the Church. In other words, the Church must be out of the way before the Anti-christ can be revealed. According to this view, the Church must be raptured before the Tribulation and the revealing of the Anti-christ (ibid., 323–324).

Comfort One Another

The Apostle Paul in 1 Thessalonians 4:15–17 states,

> For this we say to you by the word of the Lord, that we who are alive and remain until the coming of the Lord will by no means precede those who are asleep. For the Lord Himself will descend from heaven with a shout, with the voice of an archangel, and with the trumpet of God. And the dead in Christ will rise first. Then we who are alive and remain shall be caught up together with them in the clouds to meet the Lord in the air. And thus we shall always be with the Lord. Therefore comfort one another.

It would be of very little reassurance for the Apostle Paul to have said, "Comfort one another with these words" (1 Thess. 4:18) if he was telling the saints to prepare to enter the Great Tribulation and to meet the Anti-christ. I do not think that the Church will be here on earth during the time of Jacob's trouble. I do not see how the Church and the Anti-christ can coexist on the earth at the same time. God has given the Church of Jesus Christ tremendous spiritual power. If the Church was around during the reign of the Anti-christ, they would be entering into spiritual warfare against him through intercession, prayer, and fasting. This spiritual warfare would prevent the Anti-christ from deceiving people and taking control. It appears that the only way the Anti-christ is going to be free to deceive and to establish his world government, is if the Church of Jesus Christ has already been raptured. I don't think we are going to be around when the Anti-christ comes. I believe that Paul was teaching the Church to be comforted by the fact that they will escape the cruelty of the Anti-christ and the Great Tribulation.

Archeological Evidence

One of the keys to understanding the Book of Revelation is to understand the historical background that relates to the material. In Revelation 13:1–18 we read about the Beast, who is the Anti-christ, rising out of the sea. In addition, another beast who is the False Prophet will mark people with a special number that will allow them to buy or sell. The number of the beast is 666.

The Greek and Hebrew language did not have a separate numerical system. As such, all the letters of their alphabets carried a numerical value. The symbolic number of the Beast is the total of the number values in the letters of his name. He is a counterfeit Trinity who wages war against the true trinity of the Father, Son, and Holy Spirit. However, in order to understand this passage of Scripture, it is helpful to understand the historical context of the passage. In the *Biblical Archeological Review*, Steven Friesen gives us the historical background from archeological research on this passage (Steven Friesen, "Ephesus—Key to a Vision in Revelation," *Biblical Archeological Review* [May/June 1993]: 25–37).

According to Friesen, archeology tells us a great deal about Roman emperor worship and what John was attempting to tell us in the Book of Revelation. The ancient city of Ephesus is a key to unlocking the Book of Revelation. Ephesus, which was located in western Asia Minor, was located in relative near proximity to six other important cities. Ephesus, Smyrna, Pergamos, Thyatira, Sardis, Philadelphia, and Laodicea were the cities where the seven churches of the Apocalypse were located in Revelation 1:20.

The second-century Christian writer Irenaeus stated that the Book of Revelation first appeared at the end of the Roman emperor Domitian's reign. Many scholars believe that Revelation 13 is a critical description of the worship of Roman emperors in Asia Minor. The first beast who rises from the sea represents Rome who is empowered by Satan. The second beast is an ally of the first beast who exercises Rome's authority and causes people to worship Rome.

During this period of history part of the official religion of Rome which was sponsored by the state was the worship of the various Roman emperors. These cults of Rome made people worship emperors like Julius Caesar. In the city of Ephesus there was a large boulevard called the Arcadian Way, which was connected to a massive twenty-four thousand seat theater. This was the site of a riot when the Apostle Paul spoke in Acts 19:23–41, where the local cult of the fertility goddess Artemis attacked Paul. Also, in Ephesus was the Temple of the Sebastoi which comes from the word *revered* in Greek. This temple was dedicated to the worship of the Roman emperors Vespasian (A.D. 69–79), Titius (A.D. 79–81), and Domitian (A.D. 81–96).

The construction of this temple gives us some insight into what the ancient Romans believed. The colonnade on the second level of the temple featured the sculptured statues of their various gods and goddesses. These deities supported and protected the temple in which the emperors were worshiped. In a sense, the symbolism of the temple communicated the message that the power of Rome and of the individual Roman emperors came from their various gods. To a large degree, this was a correct analysis of the situation. These gods were the symbolic expression of actual demon powers and territorial spirits. Without realizing it, the Romans were acknowledging the fact that their power stemmed from the influence of principalities and powers. Rome was a kingdom that was not built on God's power but rather the powers of darkness.

Originally, scholars believed that the Temple of the Sebastoi was simply dedicated to the Emperor Titus. But, recent archeological evidence reveals that it was dedicated to more than one emperor. What this reveals is that John, in Revelation, was not just denouncing the Emperor Domitian, but the entire system of imperial cults, which were the very foundation of the social and political order of Rome. In ancient Rome the people literally worshiped their emperors along with various gods and goddesses.

On one level the Book of Revelation declared that Rome who was the beast from the sea was not really ruled by earthly emperors. These earthly rulers were puppets of Satanic power. According to John, the very foundation of Roman civilization was based on idolatry and blasphemy which were enforced through violence and the persecution of those who sought to live a godly life.

The time is coming when a future Anti-christ, or Beast, will rise again, and the people who live in the world system will worship this beast. The Beast will gain his power from Satan himself. The Bible is telling us that this entire world system is being propped up by Satanic power. The mass media, the political system, entertainment, education, and science is rooted in idolatry and blasphemy, and like ancient Rome it is increasingly persecuting those who seek to live a godly life.

History is moving toward its climax. There will be a revival of the ancient Roman Empire in the last days whose ruler will be the Anti-christ. Behind this movement and undergirding the economic, political, and cultural realities will be the powers of darkness. For a brief season this dark Anti-christ system will flower with grotesque seductiveness upon the earth. Then at the appointed time, God will put an end to it and set up His kingdom which will reign forever and ever, amen.

Chapter Six

When the Anti-christ Comes

The world is ripe for the emergence of a charismatic world leader that the Bible calls the Anti-christ. The Anti-christ is not going to come in the form of a screaming madman like Adolf Hitler. We live in a time of what communications theorist Marshall McLuhan called the "cool medium." This means that because of mass media like television, VCRs, satellite, the information highway, and global communications network, the Anti-christ is going to be someone who is able to present himself well through the media.

Imagine someone who could be a combination of the late John F. Kennedy, Tony Robbins, and L. Ron Hubbard, except that this person would be totally possessed and energized by Satan. The Anti-christ will be charming, charismatic, alluring, compelling, seductive, and totally evil. He will have the power to seduce the world away from Jesus Christ in order to follow him.

The Anti-christ will not come like some Charles Manson-type, foaming at the mouth and shouting. The Anti-christ is going to be rational, articulate, intelligent, likeable, and able to convince the people of the world that he is the Messiah. The Anti-christ will communicate with the entire population of earth through a global satellite interlink.

When Evangelist Billy Graham preached his Global Mission crusade to over one billion people in over 175 countries via satellite from Puerto Rico, he made the comment that this powerful technology could one day be used by the Anti-christ to deceive the world. Can you imagine a time when giant screen televisions in sports stadiums across the world will be used to bring the deceptive message of the Anti-christ to billions of people? Just think of places like Times Square, New York, and Red Square being jammed with people who have gathered to hear a false message of hope from the Great Deceiver.

Think of the millions of households who will be tuned in through tiny satellite dishes and large screen high definition televisions who will sit mesmerized to the message of the Anti-christ whose smooth words will echo in surround sound in living rooms all across the planet.

If you think that this sounds too far-fetched to be true then just look at recent history. When dictators like Chairman Mao of China, Lenin of Russia, and Fidel Castro of Cuba seized control of their nations, they launched massive cultural revolutions. Their faces adorned giant posters on city walls, and the people would worship these evil men. Chairman Mao ordered his soldiers to burn Bibles and instead began to distribute his little red book called *The Quotations of Chairman Mao.* During these revolutions, televisions were not in every home. Just think of how much more pervasive these revolutions would have been if they had been able to use television.

The people in our nation are not immune from this kind of worship. Masses of young people live empty lives and are eager to follow any new pop idol. Superstars like Madonna and Michael Jackson can jam massive stadiums around the globe, and their faces are everywhere from TV screens to T-shirts, coffee mugs, magazines, and jackets. Just imagine what will happen when people begin to follow the Anti-christ with the same devotion they give to entertainment superstars.

The people who are alive on earth will literally worship the Anti-christ. They will wear jackets, T-shirts, and hats with his face and name written on them. The Anti-christ's face will be on magazine covers, books, and giant computer generated billboards in every major city.

The people of earth will be gripped by a powerful delusion, and a kind of mass hysteria will sweep society. During the 1960s and early 1970s a kind of hysteria gripped the minds of an entire generation that began to revolt against their parents' values and society. The counterculture was born, and people began to take drugs, engage in promiscuous sex, and get involved in Eastern mysticism. Like many of you, I was involved in that counterculture. There was a kind of madness that had taken over. But, this will be nothing compared to the insanity that will come upon people who follow the Anti-christ.

The Lawless One

In 2 Thessalonians 2:1–11 the Apostle Paul warns of the coming Anti-christ who is called various names such as "the man of sin," "the son of perdition," and the "lawless one." Around 167 B.C. an evil ruler named Antiochus Epiphanes desecrated the temple in Jerusalem. Antiochus Epiphanes placed an image of his chief god Zeus Olympus, fashioned as a man, with a face that looked like Antiochus himself, and placed it in the Holy of Holies. He then commanded the Jewish people to worship it at the penalty of death.

This horrible episode in Jewish history, which is recorded in the Book of Maccabees, points to a future time when the Anti-christ will step into the temple of God and demand that the entire human race worship him. The Apostle Paul talks about this future event when he says:

> Let no one deceive you by any means; for that Day will not come unless the falling away comes first, and the man of sin is revealed, the son of perdition, who opposes and exalts himself above all that is called God or that is worshipped, so that he sits as God in the temple of God, showing himself that he is God. (2 Thess. 2:3–4)

> And the lawless one will be revealed, whom the
> Lord will consume with the breath of His mouth
> and will destroy with the brightness of His coming.
> The coming of the lawless one is according to the
> working of Satan, with all power, signs and lying
> wonders, and with all unrighteous deception among
> those who perish, because they did not receive the
> love of the truth, that they might be saved. And for
> this reason God will send them strong delusion,
> that they should believe the lie. (2 Thess. 2:8–11)

In this passage of Scripture the Apostle Paul is talking
about the coming Anti-christ and how he will deceive
millions of people on earth. Daniel prophesied regarding
the coming of the Anti-christ when he said,

> And forces shall be mustered by him, and they shall
> defile the sanctuary fortress; then they shall take
> away the daily sacrifices, and place there the abomi-
> nation of desolation. Those who do wickedly against
> the covenant he shall corrupt with flattery; but the
> people who know their God shall be strong and
> carry out great exploits. And those of the people
> who understand shall instruct many; yet for many
> days they shall fall by the sword and flame, by
> captivity and plundering. Now when they fall, they
> shall be aided with a little help; but many shall join
> them with intrigue. And some of those of under-
> standing shall fall, to refine them, purify them, and
> make them white, until the time of the end; be-
> cause it is still for an appointed time. Then the
> king shall do according to his own will: he shall
> exalt and magnify himself above every god, shall
> speak blasphemies against the God of gods, and
> shall prosper till the wrath has been accomplished;
> for what has been determined shall be done.
> (Dan.11:31–36)

Here in the late sixth century B.C. Daniel gives us an
amazing prophecy about the end of time and the work of
the Anti-christ. This passage of Scripture teaches us that

the temple of God will be rebuilt and the daily sacrifices restored. Then, when the Anti-christ comes he will do away with the sacrifices and shall demand that people worship him instead of God.

Daniel is talking about the same event as the Apostle Paul. Paul warns us that the coming of the Anti-christ will be accompanied by the "working of Satan , with all power, signs and lying wonders" (2 Thess. 2:9). If you ever look at old black and white news footage and see film of Adolf Hitler speaking to hundreds of thousands of people, it is obvious that these people thought that Hitler was a god. They were caught up in a powerful spell and delusion that Hitler generated.

Paul tells us that when people reject the truth of Jesus Christ, they are ripe for deception. Have you ever watched the television news or C-SPAN 1 or C-SPAN 2 on cable when a politician was speaking and wondered how anybody could believe this guy? People who do not know the truth of God's Word seem not to have any spiritual discernment. Yet, when the Anti-christ comes people will be deceived by a very powerful and strong delusion. In a sense, the Anti-christ will be allowed to mesmerize them and totally deceive them.

In addition, Paul talks about the "mystery of lawlessness" that is at work in the world. The mystery of lawlessness is the increasing power of evil and sin in the last days. The Bible teaches us that in the heart of every man and woman, who does not know Jesus Christ as their Lord and Savior, is the corrupting force of sin. As we approach the end of time, we are going to see the evil in man's heart come to the surface as never before.

Right now on this earth there is a restraining force that Paul mentioned in 2 Thessalonians 2:7 that is causing evil to be kept in check. Although Bible scholars differ as to what this restraining force is, I believe that the restraining force is the presence of the Holy Spirit at work in the world. Despite the fact that we are seeing increasing evil in our world today, the presence of Jesus

Christ in the lives of individual Christians and the prayers of God's people release the Holy Spirit and the power of God in our society. If that force and presence of the Holy Spirit were removed, then all hell would break loose. The Church of Jesus Christ is the only thing keeping the forces of darkness in restraint here on this planet. If the Church of Jesus Christ was to be raptured, then this restraining force would basically be removed except for people who accept Christ after the rapture.

Mass Hypnosis

One may well ask, "Why would anyone follow the Anti-christ?" Tragically, the Bible tells us that when men deliberately exchange the truth for a lie that they will believe anything. Romans 1:28 states, "And even as they did not like to retain God in their knowledge, God gave them over to a debased mind, to do those things which are not fitting." In this passage Paul is specifically speaking about the sin of homosexuality and how its practice can lead to a debased mind. Yet, he uncovers the important truth that when men reject the truth of God, they are open to any lie.

We are warned in 1 John 4:1–6,

> Beloved, do not believe every spirit, but test the spirits, whether they are of God; because many false prophets have gone out into the world. By this you know the Spirit of God: Every spirit that confesses that Jesus Christ has come in the flesh is of God, and every spirit that does not confess that Jesus Christ has come in the flesh is not of God. And this is the spirit of the Anti-Christ, which you have heard was coming, and is now already in the world. You are of God, little children, and have overcome them, because He who is in you is greater then he who is in the world. They are of the world. Therefore they speak as of the world, and the world hears them. We are of God. He who knows God hears us; he who is not of God does not hear us. By

this we know the spirit of truth and the spirit of error.

There are many voices of the Anti-christ in our world. Clearly, the New Age movement and occult religions speak with voices that contradict God's Word. However, there are now many voices inside our government and media that promote philosophies that are in direct opposition to the kingdom of God. The danger is that as more and more people who have lifestyles and belief systems that are antagonistic to a Judeo-Christian world view become part of our government, they are going to use that power to persecute the Church.

Any voice that speaks against God's teachings that are outlined in the Bible is an Anti-christ voice. The Holy Spirit and the inner voice of their God-given conscience warns people before they enter error and deception. However, individuals and a nation may choose to ignore that warning voice.

When I was involved in what could be called the New Age movement at the University of Missouri, I regularly read the books of an American guru called Stephen Gaskin who taught about mental telepathy and traveling up and down the astral plane of higher consciousness. One day Stephen Gaskin came to the University of Missouri with many of his followers from their commune called The Farm in Tennessee.

I remember meeting Gaskin who was sporting a purple outfit and long hair and a beard looking something like a psychedelic Jesus. He emanated a presence and charisma that was supernatural. Some of my friends, who were psychology students going for their doctorates, were so overwhelmed by this man that they were going to move to Tennessee to live on The Farm commune.

However, when I met Gaskin, I had a powerful spiritual experience. I sensed what can only be described as a kind of telepathic communication with the man on a higher spiritual plane. I could feel the spiritual energy pouring out of this man. Yet, deep within me I felt an unrest, and I sensed that something was not right here. A voice warned me not to open myself up to Stephen Gaskin, and I told him that something was not right.

I realized later that it was the voice of the Holy Spirit that was warning me about a danger. God was giving me a choice, and I could have ignored God's voice and surrendered to spiritual deception. In the same way, nations and individuals are warned by God and can either ignore that warning or heed it. If they ignore God's warning, then they are given over to total delusion and deception.

Germany in Adolf Hitler's time was repeatedly warned both individually and as a nation. Yet, the masses chose to ignore the warnings, and they came under the spell of an anti-christ spirit. The day is coming when the Antichrist is going to charm the world with his seductive lies. But, he is not just going to take over. Individuals, nations, and the world as a whole will be given many warnings by God, and they will make many little choices along the road to destruction.

Prozac as Sorcery

How is it possible to control millions of people worldwide? How will the Anti-christ be able to deceive billions on earth? In the classic novel *Brave New World* the people are brainwashed and controlled by a drug called soma. A couple of decades ago the CIA conducted its infamous MK-Ultra experiments with LSD. In fact, Ken Kesey got the idea for his novel *One Flew over the Cuckoo's Nest* after ingesting LSD as part of a government experiment. Kesey later drove around the country in a psychedelic bus called Further and turned people on to LSD through what was called the Electric Kool-Aid Acid Test.

In the 1960s pharmacology produced a pharmacopeia of mind-expanding drugs. Now in the 1990s mind-altering drugs have gone legitimate with names like Prozac, Paxil, Zoloft and Effexor. According to *Newsweek*, the drug Prozac racked up $1.2 billion in sales, and Paxil $250 million; Zoloft $457 million, and other antidepressants

$1.2 billion (Geoffrey Cowely, "Beyond Prozac," *Newsweek* [7 February 1994]: 42). These statistics coupled with a multi-billion dollar illegal drug trade and an alcohol industry that generates billions of dollars, implies that America is literally stoned out of its mind. To use the words of the late Jim Morrison, of the rock group, the Doors, who died of a heart attack which many believe was induced by alcohol or drugs, America is "stoning in the neon." Is it no wonder that our society is out of control because it's out of its mind?

In Revelation, 9:21 we read, "And they did not repent of their murders or their sorceries or their sexual immorality or their thefts." The word *sorceries* comes from the Greek word *pharmakeia* from which we get our modern words *pharmacy* and *pharmacist* and describes the use of drugs, medicine, or spells. Later the word was used to mean poisoning and then sorcery along with drugs, incantations, charms, and magic (Spirit Filled Life Bible, Thomas Nelson Publishers, page 1,973).

The Book of Revelation describes a world that is immersed in drugs and a world that will not repent of its drugs even in the face of apocalypse. The reason the Anti-christ will be able to grab control is because billions of people in our world live in an altered state of consciousness due to street drugs, alcohol, mysticism, and legal drugs like Prozac. Consequently, they have lost all real discernment because they are high.

When masses of people are on drugs, they can be easily manipulated and lied to. The widespread use of drugs and legal mind benders like Prozac are paving the way for mass conditioning. Like Pavlov's dog who was taught to salivate with the ringing of a bell, the masses can be conditioned to obey any voice once their senses have been dulled.

Chapter Seven

The Anti-christ Deception

The Book of Revelation talks about a day when billions of people will be deceived into worshiping the Anti-christ. One of the responsibilities of the False Prophet will be to cause people to worship the Anti-christ. Satan has been interested in stealing the worship people give to God for himself since the beginning of time. This is why 2 Thessalonians 2:3–4 states, "Let no one deceive you by any means; for that Day will not come unless the falling away comes first, and the man of sin is revealed, the son of perdition, who opposes and exalts himself above all that is worshipped, so that he sits as God in the temple of God, showing himself that he is God."

Satan through the Anti-christ wants to get people to worship him. One of the main ways that he plans to do this is through deception and the establishment of a false religion. In 1 John 4:1–3 and 5-6, we are warned by John about false religion:

> Beloved, do not believe every spirit, but test the spirits, whether they are of God; because many false prophets have gone out into the world. By this you know the Spirit of God: Every spirit that confesses Jesus Christ has come in the flesh is of God, and every spirit that does not confess that Jesus Christ has come in the flesh is not of God. And this is the spirit of the Anti-christ, which you have heard was coming, and is now already in the world....They are of the world. Therefore they speak as of the world, and the world hears them. We are of God.

He who knows God hears us; he who is not of God
does not hear us. By this we know the spirit of truth
and the spirit of error.

Any religious or spiritual teaching that attempts to tell
mankind that it is possible to be made right with God
other than through faith in Christ is an "anti-christ" religion. The Old Testament would not fit into this cat-
egory because it teaches men to place their faith in God's
blood covenant and points specifically to Jesus Christ as
the Messiah.

The Spirit of the Anti-christ

The Apostle John warns us in John 2:18, "Little children, it is the last hour; and as you have heard that the
Anti-christ is coming, even now many anti-christs have
come, by which we know that it is the last hour." The
Bible teaches us that there is going to be an embodiment
of evil in a world ruler called the Anti-christ and that
there is a spirit of the Anti-christ at work in the world.
The founder of CBN, Pat Robertson, writes,

> Remember that the anti-christ spirit is anybody who
> tries to draw people away from Jesus, saying, "Wor-
> ship me." The anti-christ spirit is often present now
> in the worship and veneration we give to govern-
> ments, dictators, military leaders, and various hu-
> man figures. Systems being taught in our schools,
> media, and intellectual circles are often much like
> that which will ultimately lead people to the Anti-
> christ, because he will be the consummate figure of
> humanism. (Pat Robertson, "Spiritual Answers to
> Hard Questions," Spirit Filled Life Bible, Thomas
> Nelson Publishers)

When a political leader, guru, spiritual teacher, religion, philosophy, or belief system rises up which is in
direct opposition to the teachings of Jesus Christ, this
person or movement is being energized by a very real
"spirit of the Anti-christ." People who seem to have un-
usual charisma or personal magnetism and who draw

people into evil are being empowered by the forces of darkness.

It is important that when we look at history or current events that we recognize that there is a very real spiritual dimension to what is going on. The amazing power that men like Adolf Hitler, a cult leader, or political personality can have over people is due to spiritual energy. If we don't take the reality of the invisible realm and spiritual reality into the equation then we cannot fully explain why certain leaders, entertainers, and religious figures can rise so prominently to the top.

Adolf Hitler and the Occult

When you learned about Adolf Hitler and the Nazi party in school, you were not told the most important facts regarding Hitler's mysterious rise to power. Adolf Hitler was not just a political leader; he was deeply involved in the occult, and key leaders in the Nazi party and the Third Reich were practicing Satanists. In fact, Hitler belonged to the same powerful occult circle that leading German judges, police chiefs, lawyers, university professors, aristocrats, bankers, industrialists, scientists, surgeons, and businessmen belonged to.

Although Hitler deliberately concealed his ties to the occult in his book *Mein Kamp*, the reality is that the committee and the original forty members of the New German Worker's party from which the Nazi party evolved were all members of the most powerful occult society in Germany, which was financed by the High Command— the Thule Gesellschaft. This Thule group was a powerful and secretive group that controlled many aspects of Bavarian society from terrorist operations to murder.

One of the key leaders of this group was a man named Dietrich Eckhart, who was a dedicated Satanist and adept in the arts and rituals of Black Magic. Eckhart believed he was on a spiritual mission from Satan to prepare the vessel of the Anti-christ who would be inspired by Lucifer and lead the Aryan race to glory. Eckhart was convinced that Adolf Hitler was this vessel of the Anti-christ who would be used by Satan to conquer the world. Eckhart said, "Follow Hitler! He will dance, but it is I who have called the tune! I have initiated him into the 'Secret Doctrine,' opened his centers of vision and given him the means to communicate with the Powers" (Trevor Ravenscroft, *The Spear of Destiny* [York Beach, Maine: Samuel Weiser, Inc., 1991], 91).

Adolf Hitler used a powerful psychedelic drug similar in substance to mescaline and LSD. The use of this psychedelic drug allowed Hitler to achieve his goal of possession by Lucifer. It opened him up to powerful occult and evil powers that would help him seduce Germany. Through years of occult involvement and mind-altering drugs, Adolf Hitler willfully prepared himself to be "a chalice for the Spirit of the Anti-christ" (ibid., 25, 77–78, 80–84).

After being influenced by what is called the Secret Doctrine (which taught that the Aryan people were led out of Atlantis by the sons of God or supermen under the symbol of the Sun Wheel or Four-Armed Swastika), *The Secret Doctrine* was written by Madame Blavatsky, who gave long descriptions of the vanished civilizations of Atlantis. Blavatsky's *The Secret Doctrine* still influences people like New Age spokeswomen Shirley Maclaine and Marriane Williamson.

It is clear that Adolf Hitler's rise to power was not just an accident. Hitler literally made a pact with the devil in order to gain supernatural powers. The alarming thing is that even though the Third Reich was destroyed, there continues to exist today secret occult and Satanist groups that are quite active in our society. Perhaps somewhere on the planet the real Anti-christ is being prepared for a global takeover.

I think it would be naive not to fully understand that in our world today there exist secret organizations that are part of an active occult conspiracy. We must remember that there is a real war going on in our world between the forces of Christ and the Anti-christ. This warfare is being conducted in the schools, the mass media, the arts, the political sphere, and even in the religious institutions of our world.

The Great Apostasy

Before the Anti-christ appears on the scene, a number of things have to take place. In 2 Thessalonians 2:1–11, the Apostle Paul writes,

> Now, brethren, concerning the coming of our Lord Jesus Christ and our gathering together to Him, we ask you, not to be soon shaken in mind or troubled either by spirit or by word or by letter, as if from us, as though the day of Christ had come. Let no one deceive you by any means: for that Day will not come unless the falling away comes first, and the man of sin is revealed, the son of perdition, who opposes and exalts himself above all that is called God or that is worshipped, so that he sits as God in the temple of God, showing that he is God. Do you not remember that when I was still with you I told you these things? And now you know what is restraining, that he may be revealed in his own time. For the mystery of lawlessness is already at work; only He who now restrains will do so until He is taken out of the way. And then the lawless one will be revealed, whom the Lord will consume with the breath of his mouth and destroy with the brightness of His coming. The coming of the lawless one is according to the working of Satan with all power, signs and lying wonders, and with all unrighteous deception among those who perish, because they did not receive the love of the truth, that they might be saved. And for this reason God will send them a strong delusion, that they should believe the lie.

In the above Scripture verses, Paul speaks of the end-time scenario that will lead to the Second Coming of Jesus Christ. Ancient Jewish history has already shown evil rulers such as Antiochus Epiphanes who, around 167

B.C., ravaged the temple at Jerusalem, as well as Roman emperors such as the morally perverse Gaius Caligula (A.D. 37–41) and Domitian (A.D. 81–96) who wanted to be God.

In Nazi Germany during the 1930s, Adolf Hitler was able to grab the reigns of power because the German people had allowed their churches and seminaries to undermine the authority of the Scripture through what was called "higher criticism," and they had lost their capacity for spiritual discernment. The Bible shows that there is a unique sociological as well as spiritual principle. When any individual or nation begins to reject truth, they open themselves up for spiritual delusion. If people will not worship God, they will find something else to worship. This principle goes back to the time of Moses. When the people rejected God, they created a golden calf to worship instead.

The warning here is that as our society continues to reject the truth of God's Word, they become vulnerable on a mass level to delusion and deception. It is in that climate of great spiritual darkness that the Anti-christ will be able to convince the world that he is "God" and maneuver a global takeover.

Verse 11 of 2 Thessalonians, chapter 2, states, "And for this reason God will send them a strong delusion, that they should believe a lie." As someone who was active in the counterculture movement in the late 1960s and who demonstrated with the radical activist Abbie Hoffman in New York City, I have seen this principle of a strong delusion at work. I have seen hundreds of thousands of people caught up in a kind of mass hypnosis and ready to be led. Psychologists have shown that people who get caught up in cults, fringe political movements, and other activities often come from more educated and affluent homes.

There are many aspects of the modern ecological, peace, and higher consciousness movements that border on a blind allegiance to creating a new world government. These activities could very easily be manipulated by the Anti-christ.

Chapter Eight

The Dream of
One-World Government

When you drive on the freeways in southern California, you often see people with bumper stickers which read, "One People One Planet" or similar things. The idea of some kind of one-world government where "one people" can live united on "one planet" has become a very popular idea. This philosophy is promoted on television shows like "Star Trek," whose founder Gene Rodenberry was a militant humanist who believed that a new golden age could be achieved by mankind once they rejected old fashioned ideas like the Ten Commandments and the Bible.

However, the idea for a one-world government can be found in the Book of Daniel: "The fourth beast shall be a fourth kingdom on earth, which shall be different from all other kingdoms" (Dan. 7:24). In this passage Daniel was talking about a future one-world government ruled by the Anti-christ.

This idea for a new world order and a one-world government has been around for a long time. In 1921 the great science fiction writer H.G. Wells, who wrote such classics as *The Invisible Man*, wrote in his book *Salvaging Civilization* (New York: Macmillan Company, 1921) about the need to create a one-world "cult" that would promote the idea of a humanist and socialist new world order with a religious fervor. Wells said, "The activities of a cult which sets itself to bring about a one world-state would at first be propagandist, then would be intellectual and educational. . . . Such a cult must direct itself particularly to the young" (p. 38).

H.G. Wells despised the Bible, and he believed passionately in one-world government. He urged that men and women become "missionaries" for a new world order, which he called a "saving doctrine." H.G. Wells outlined a master plan to gain control of the world in which people who believed in this new world order would "print and publish books, endow schools and teaching, organize the distribution of literature, insist upon the proper instruction of children in world-wide charity and fellowship, fight against every sort of suppression or restrictive control of right education . . . bring pressure through political and social channels upon every teaching organization to teach history aright, sustain missions and a new sort of missionary, the missionaries to all mankind of knowledge and the idea of *one-world civilization and one world community*" (ibid., 40, emphasis added).

H.G. Wells was calling for a one-world revolution where militant humanists would become the new missionaries that would recruit the young. Wells hated preachers and those who believed in patriotism and national sovereignty. H.G. Wells wanted to write his own version of the Bible, called *The Bible of Civilization*, where he wanted to throw away all the biblical standards for traditional morality.

H.G. Wells belonged to a group of intellectuals who planned to create this one-world government. But, the important thing to understand is that this plan to recruit young people and take over society has largely succeeded. The political correctness movement on school campuses; diversity training by large corporations like AT&T, which force their employees to attend workshops in order to accept homosexuality; and the control of the mass media by a liberal elite, who attempt to use their influence for their own agenda, is exactly the thing that Wells envisioned.

This movement towards globalism is not accidental. It

was dreamed of by groups of intellectuals and bankrolled by powerful organizations in order to create a new world order based on humanistic ideas which are often in conflict with our Judeo-Christian heritage.

Creating the New World Order

H.G. Wells used his considerable influence as a successful author to campaign for a new world order based on his humanistic ideas. With the success of books like *War of the Worlds* and *First Men in the Moon*, Wells was able to attract large numbers of people to take him very seriously. He began to write books like *The New World Order* in 1940 where he called for a socialistic superstate to run the world.

In his books, Wells promoted the idea of a Declaration of the Rights of Man, where everyone would be entitled to food, medical care, a full education, and work at the job of his choice. At first glance, these ideas sound wonderful, but when you dig deeper into them they become the nightmare they really are. Everybody knows there is no such thing as a "free lunch," and a massive global government bureaucracy would have to be created to achieve this. History shows us that whenever you build up a massive government in the "name of the people," a tyrannical government always emerges to oppress the people.

It is no accident that H.G. Wells was a socialist who belonged to The Fabian Society in England, which was named after the Roman dictator Fabius in the third century B.C., a military genius who used deceptive defensive military campaigns to win over his opponents. Men like H.G. Wells and George Bernard Shaw planned to turn England and the world into a socialist state not through revolution but evolution.

The Fabian Society was an elite group of intellectuals and businessmen who had a profound influence on the rest of society. They believed in the creation of a new world order based on socialist ideas and sought to promote these ideas in the United States as well as England. Wells wrote a book called *A Modern Utopia*, where he preached about the virtues of socialism and a "world state" where all property is collectively owned.

Yet, Wells outlined a sinister plan for world control run by elites whom he called the "creator class," and under them would be the "kinetic or engineering class," and finally the "dull and the base class" who would be controlled by the upper classes. In the Utopian world envisioned by Wells, there would be complete sexual liberty with no restrictive moral codes.

H.G. Wells also hated the Catholic church, which he criticized for being reactionary, and he criticized the Jews in what he termed "the Jewish Problem." Nevertheless, his ideas spread to educators, intellectuals, and powerful men throughout the world who had the power to put these ideas into action.

Woodrow Wilson and a One-World Order

In 1912 Woodrow Wilson, a Democrat, was elected president of the United States. Wilson was reported to be a sincere Christian who was catapulted from governor of New Jersey to president of the United States through the financial banking of the Rockefellers, Bernard Baruch, Jacob Schiff, and other wealthy financiers.

Around this time Wilson developed a close relationship with an agent of these financiers, Col. Edward Mandell House. House had just written a revolutionary political novel entitled *Philip Dru, Administrator: A Story of Tomorrow* which was the account of a dreamer who manages to become dictator of the world and establishes a one-world economic system along with one-world government. This one-world government would be run by an elite council of twelve men, with the United States leading the way to a new world order that would eventually be surrendered into the hands of this one-world government.

In *Philip Dru, Administrator: A Story of Tomorrow*, Colonel House calls for a socialist-style world-state, a Federal

Reserve Banking System, and other social legislation. Ironically, President Wilson enacted many of the things that House called for in *Philip Dru, Administrator*. Colonel House wrote this novel as a kind of road map towards a new world order and eventually a one-world government. Like the dreamer in his novel, House became incredibly powerful, influencing the policies of both Woodrow Wilson and Franklin D. Roosevelt's administration. It is no accident that Woodrow Wilson put foreword the League of Nations, which was the forerunner of the United Nations, the Federal Reserve System and the passage of the Federal Income Tax under the Internal Revenue Service.

Col. Edward Mandell House was the son of the Civil War Rothschild agent Thomas House and was a representative of the Rothschild Banks as well as a member of the Institute of International Affairs that started in Paris at the Majestic Hotel in 1919. The Institute of International Affairs became the Council on Foreign Relations in 1921. From his home in Magnolia, Massachusetts, House advised both Wilson and Roosevelt with his ideas of a one-world government.

House regularly met with powerful men like the Rockefellers, the Schiffs, the Warburgs, the Kahns, and the Morgans, who were all involved in the creation of the Federal Reserve Board. In addition, House was a founding member of the Council on Foreign Relations.

Roots of the New World Order

The philosophical ideas about a new world order were promoted through intellectual circles like The Fabian Society. However, what was needed was for these ideas to be turned into reality by men who had the money and power to make these things happen. In 1921 an organization called the Council on Foreign Relations was formed by leaders of finance and industry. This council included men like Thomas W. Lamont, who was Woodrow Wilson's financial advisor; John W. Davis, a House of Morgan lawyer; and of course the Rockefellers who funded the council.

In the beginning, the Council on Foreign Relations was totally intertwined with the oil interests of the Rockefellers and Standard Oil. It was formed to insure the pursuit of foreign oil. The Rockefeller family played a primary role in the creation of the Council on Foreign Relations. Pres. Woodrow Wilson named Raymond Fosdick as secretary general of the League of Nations, and he helped get the Rockefeller family involved in a massive realignment of global power that would take place during the next decade (Peter Collier and David Horowitz, *The Rockefellers* [New York: Holt, Rinehart, and Winston, 1976], 134, 142).

With the creation of the Council on Foreign Relations, which later became the Trilateral Commission, the plans for a new world order were being put in place. John Davison Rockefeller was a prime mover in the Council on Foreign Relations (CFR), and he helped establish the National Council of Churches in 1950, which has promoted ultraliberal causes and merged twelve Protestant missionary organizations.

The Rockefeller family believed that organizations like the National Council of Churches and earlier Federal Council of Churches could play an important part in laying out this new world order. In 1917 while speaking at the Baptist Social Union, Rockefeller said, "Would that I had the power to bring to your minds the vision as it unfolds before me! I see all denominational emphasis set aside. . . . I see the church molding the thought of the world as it has never done before, leading all great movements as it should. I see it literally establishing the Kingdom of God on earth" (ibid., 151).

Perhaps, without realizing it, Rockefeller was painting an accurate picture of the future rule of the Antichrist, where a false church would motivate people to worship a false Christ. The Church was never called to establish the kingdom of God on earth through humanistic programs. Only Jesus Christ can establish the kingdom of God on earth when He returns during His Second Advent.

It is important to understand that the church that Rockefeller wanted to see establish the kingdom of God on earth was not a Bible-based Christian church. Rockefeller's own pastor was the Reverend Harry Emerson Fosdick, pastor of the old First Presbyterian Church who once delivered a sermon entitled "Shall The Fundamentalists Win?" which attacked "fundamentalist Christians" who believed the Bible literally.

When Rockefeller spent over $26 million building the famous Riverside Church in New York, the main portal of the church contained figures of Confucious, Hegel, Mohammed, and even Charles Darwin. Rockefeller believed in humanism and not orthodox Christianity. When the Rockefeller family began to finance the Council on Foreign Relations, the World Council of Churches, and the United Nations in order to build a new world order, the new world order they had in mind was one based on man and not God. Essentially, it was an anti-christ movement because it promoted the idea that man apart from Jesus Christ can be his own savior.

Chapter Nine

The United Nations

In January of 1943 a secret steering committee for the planning of the United Nations was created by Secretary of War Cordell Hull. The committee was called the Agenda Group and was composed solely of members of the Council on Foreign Relations, with the exception of Hull, and it worked fist in glove with the United States State Department. In 1943 the Agenda Group successfully laid the groundwork for the United Nations, which would become an international organization to maintain global peace and security.

In 1945 the U.N. was officially founded, and in recent years it has mobilized an international army that has been active in Operation Desert Storm, Rwanda, Somalia, Haiti, Bosnia, and many other global "hot points." However, in recent days there has been some dangerous trends developing at the U.N. under the leadership of U.N. Secretary Gen. Boutros Boutros Ghali.

In 1994 the United Nations released its Human Development Report, which called for the expansion of the U.N.'s power. This UNDP report called for a U.N. World Court, a World Treasury, a U.N. police force, a World Bank, and other new world institutions that would be funded by some kind of global tax bill. In addition, in 1979, 176 nations signed the U.N. Convention on the Rights of the Child, which has been heavily promoted by Hillary Clinton, who announced that the U.S. ambassador to the U.N. would sign the treaty. And, it is currently being pushed in the U.S. House and the Senate.

It is clear that the powerful people who hold a humanistic world view want to use the U.N. and the courts to force parents to raise their children according to their value system, which includes the wholesale rejection of Christianity, the acceptance of homosexuality, and New Age ideas.

What Does the Trilateral Commission Want?

One often hears the phrases "shadow government" or the "invisible elite" regarding the individuals or groups who appear to run our nation from behind the scenes. One of these groups that has been very influential in setting American foreign policy is an organization called the Trilateral Commission, or the Council on Foreign Relations (CFR). Although their existence is hardly a secret (they are listed in the Yellow Pages), they have a great deal of influence on the way our government runs things, especially when it comes to things like foreign policy.

Nobody seems to know for sure how powerful these groups are. In many respects, they remind me of the old *Richie Rich* comic books, where a little rich kid had billions of dollars to play with and he bought himself swimming pools, ice cream parlors, toy factories, friends, and anything he wanted. Some of the guys who created the Trilateral Commission and the CFR are a lot like Richie Rich, except these guys buy whole nations, presidents, and entire industries. They seem to want to buy everything on the "Monopoly" board of life or treat the world like a giant game of "Risk," where the winner gets to conquer the world. But, the real world and the people in it are not toys and playthings, and there are real consequences to their actions.

The Trilateral Commission may not be like Darth Vader in the *Star Wars* trilogy who represents the "dark side of the force." However, they are an elite group who represent the interests of powerful individuals and multinational corporations. The problem is that the goals of this elite group, especially when it comes to building a global government, are often in conflict with the desires of the American people. The danger is that these groups represent a largely invisible elite and not the ordinary citizens of our nation. Our nation was originally formed as a democracy for and by the people. But, more often than not, our government is now representing powerful corporations and special interest groups that have the money to buy votes and politicians. The great filmmaker Frank Capra touched on this in his movie *Mr. Smith Goes to Washington* starring Jimmy Stewart.

In the book *The Crisis of Democracy—A Report on the Governability of Democracies to the Trilateral Commission* (Samuel P. Huntington and Joji Watanuki [New York: New York University Press, 1975]), the guiding philosophy of the Trilateral Commission is explained in somewhat cogent terms. "Democratic government does not necessarily function in a self-sustaining or self-correcting equilibrium fashion. It may instead function to give rise to outside forces and tendencies which, if unchecked by some outside agency, will eventually lead to the undermining of democracy" (p. 8).

The key phrase here is "unchecked by some outside agency." In other words, the Trilateral Commission believes that too much freedom and democracy is a bad thing and that it must be "checked by some outside agency." What this is really saying is that a democracy such as the United States cannot be run by the people, but should be instead run by an elite group such as the Trilateral Commission. This is a very dangerous thing and is exactly what our Founding Fathers wanted to protect us from when they wrote the Constitution and the Bill of Rights.

In a chapter entitled "The United States," Samuel P. Huntington, a professor of government at Harvard University and founder and editor of the Council on Foreign

Relations journal *Foreign Affairs*, writes, "We have come to recognize that there are potentially desirable limits to economic growth. There are potentially desirable limits to the indefinite expansion of political democracy. Democracy will have a longer life if it has a more balanced existence" (Samuel P. Huntington and Joji Watanuki, *The Crisis of Democracy—A Report on the Governability of Democracies to the Trilateral Commission* [New York: New York University Press, 1975]: 8). What this is really saying is that the people behind the new world order plan to restrict your freedom and your economic growth for "your own good." In a nutshell, it is a microcosm of what is going on in our nation at this very moment as an invisible elite seeks to control society through the mass media, the educational system, and the political arena against the will of the American public as expressed through the electoral process.

The Hidden Agenda

The Trilateral Commission has been operating in American politics since 1918 when it was called the Council on Foreign Relations. During World War II the Council on Foreign Relations played a key role in constructing a post-World War II international and economic order. Through billions of dollars in economic assistance and programs like the Marshall Plan and the North Atlantic Treaty Organization (NATO), Western Europe and Japan were brought into what is called "constructive accord," a term that means they are now following the game plan of the CFR.

The CFR set up an organization called the World Bank and the International Monetary Fund (IMF) to create a global trade system that became known as the Bretton Woods System after Bretton Woods, New Hampshire, where it was created. In 1954, a European organization called the Bilderberg Group, consisting of the heads of state and leaders from the United States, Europe, and Canada, began to work closely with the CFR. The

Bilderberg Group got its name from the Bilderberg Hotel in Oosterbeek, Holland, where the first meeting was held.

The Bilderberg Group has as its members key executives from powerful multinational corporations as well as political leaders. According to Peter Thompson of the London Collective, "When the Bilderberg participants form a consensus about what it is to be done, they have at their disposal powerful transnational and national instruments for bringing about what is they want to come to pass" (Holly Sklar, ed., *Trilateralism—The Trilateral Commission and Elite Planning for World Management* [Boston: South End Press, 1980], 157). Thompson also stated that groups like the Trilateral Commission, the CFR, and the Bilderberg Group have set foreign, economic, and monetary policies for many nations.

The CFR and other groups played a key role in reconstructing Europe after World War II and setting the early stages for the new world order. As early as the 1920s powerful economic leaders in the United States pushed for a "United States of Europe." However, the Great Depression of the 1930s popped the balloon on these plans and contributed to the rise of Adolf Hitler.

After the fall of Hitler, European reconstruction was developed by these groups. The Marshall Plan introduced by Secretary of State George C. Marshall in 1947 was approved by Congress for $17 billion in aid for European recovery. Out of this plan, the EEC or European Economic Community, which is called the Common Market, was established in 1957 in an act called the Rome Treaty, which was designed to eliminate market barriers in Europe. This Rome Treaty set the stage for what is now United Europe and may also play a key role in the fulfillment of biblical prophecy, which speaks of the revival of the Roman Empire and a United European Confederacy.

Daniel, chapter 7, prophecies a ten nation European confederacy that will be ruled by the Anti-christ. It is interesting to note that this United States of Europe, which has been created by a powerful group of internationalists

and globalists, could well be the revived Roman Empire
that Daniel saw in his vision.

Who's Really Running the Country?

If you are like me you may wonder why every time we
have a new president our foreign policy and everything
else remains pretty much the same. It is important to
understand that, although you were taught in school that
America is a democracy, that statement is not completely
true. It is true that the American people have been give
the power to vote by our Founding Fathers. The Repub-
lican landslide of 8 November 1994 showed that the
people's vote still does count. However, there are powerful forces in this country and around the world, which
exist behind the scenes and are attempting to control our
world. It seems that the creation of a third party is one
way that a hidden elite can do an end-run around the will
of the people. Third parties can divert much needed
votes from a particular candidate, and they can be used
to insure that a desired political candidate wins.

In 1919, an organization was created called the American Council on Foreign Relations. This council was organized by a man named Colonel E.M. House, who was a
powerful figure in the administration of Woodrow Wilson. This American Council on Foreign Relations evolved
into the CFR, or the Council on Foreign Relations, which
has now become the Trilateral Commission.

In 1939 the Council on Foreign Relations began to
control the policies of the U.S. State Department in matters of security armaments, economics, politics, and territorial problems. The Rockefeller Foundation bankrolled
this movement, and today the Council on Foreign Relations, or the Trilateral Commission, charts the course for
U.S. foreign (and much of our domestic) policy. Former
Senator Barry Goldwater quoted Rear Admiral Chester
Ward of the U.S. Navy and member of the CFR as saying,
"The most powerful clique in these elitist groups have
one objective in common—they want to bring the surren-

der of sovereignty and the national independence of the United States" (Barry M. Goldwater, *With No Apologies* [New York: Berkeley Books, 1979], 292).

It's easy to dismiss this kind of information as "conspiracy nut" stuff. Yet, my personal research has shown me that America is basically governed by a kind of invisible elite. It's not all-powerful, and they don't control everything; but they have tremendous influence in our nation and world. Even a casual observer of U.S. politics can see the way that people who don't fit into the cookie-cutter mold of this elite are systematically attacked and ridiculed. Former Vice President Dan Quayle was viciously attacked in the press because he had ideas that did not conform to their agenda. Newt Gingrich, who is a conservative and who has called for prayer in schools and the closing down of the Corporation for Public Broadcasting, which he labels "the sandbox for the rich," has been under an all-out assault from the press from the moment he has taken office.

The late Sen. Barry Goldwater had some interesting comments to make regarding the CFR when he said,

> It may be that if the CFR vision of the future could be realized, there would be a reduction in wars, a lessening of poverty, a more efficient utilization of the world's resources. To my mind, this would inevitably be accompanied by a loss in personal freedom of choice and the reestablishment of restraints which provoked the American Revolution.

Goldwater continued by saying,

> In my view, the Trilateral Commission represents a skillful, coordinated effort to seize control and consolidate the four centers of power—political, monetary, intellectual and ecclesiastical. . . . What the Trilaterals truly intend is the creation of a worldwide economic power superior to the political movements of the nation-states involved. They believe the abundant materialism they propose to

create will overwhelm existing differences. As managers and creators of the system they will rule the future. (Barry M. Goldwater, *With No Apologies* [New York: Berkeley Books, 1979], 292, 297, 299)

What's Going On?

Author Gary Kah gave an outline of how the Council on Foreign Relations has gradually become part of our government since 1920. In Kah's book *En Route to Global Occupation* (Lafayette, La.: Huntington House, 1992), he explains the history of how this has occurred.

- A number of U.S. leaders have belonged to the Council On Foreign Relations.

- Since 1920, fifteen of twenty-one treasury secretaries have been CFR members.

- Since 1944, twelve of the last fourteen secretaries of state have been CFR members.

- Since 1953, ten of thirteen national security advisors have been members of the CFR.

- Since 1953, eleven of the twelve secretaries of defense have been members of the CFR.

According to Kah's research, that totals sixty U.S. leaders of whom forty-eight have been CFR members, which is about 80 percent. In the Clinton administration, the total of CFR members in these key positions is around 100 percent. There are approximately five hundred CFR members in the Clinton administration. The Council on Foreign Relations has about three thousand members of which 15 percent hold key positions in Washington, D.C.

On the national program "This Week in Bible Prophecy," Gary Kah explains,

I ask you how would the media respond if say 80% of the top position holders of the executive office of the President over the last 50 years had been members of the Southern Baptist Convention. I believe they would cry conspiracy probably every day until something was done to correct it and yet we see no one in the media being concerned about the fact that so many people in the Administration belong to the same organization. In fact, it is fair to say that the Executive office of the President is controlled by the CFR, any other statement would be inaccurate. (Gary Kah, interview on "This Week in Bible Prophecy," 4 May 1995)

Time Warps and Frankenstein

Many people in our society do not believe that the Bible is the Word of God. They think it may contain some good things to say, but they do not believe that it is true when it comes to science, history, mathematics, physics, biology, and other areas. The Bible is different then every other book ever written in that it was written by God through men and it is true in every area that it discusses. I know this is a little hard for some people to swallow. But, the fact is that the Bible is true not only spiritually, but when it comes to science, psychology, and history as well.

There really was an Adam and Eve, a Garden of Eden, a Noah's Ark, the parting of the Red Sea, a giant whale that swallowed Jonah, a virgin birth of the Messiah, the miracle of the loaves and fishes, demons being cast out of people, miraculous healings, and the death and resurrection of Jesus Christ. To top it all off, Jesus Christ is coming again, just like He said, to establish a new heaven and new earth.

Some people are intimidated by modern science and think that the Bible will not stand up to the light of hard scientific evidence. Nothing could be further from the truth. The God of the Bible is an omniscient and super-intelligent Being who understands the complexities of modern physics, who can unravel the genetic code in microseconds, and who was responsible for the design and function of the entire universe. Incredibly, modern

man has the arrogance to look at the universe and deny
the existence of its Creator.

Unfortunately, many of the leaders of our day have
been educated in secular universities that have indoctri-
nated them into a humanistic world view. They come out
of these schools with a very limited understanding about
life and make decisions out of a very narrow context.
Even many so called born-again Christians who entered
the field of politics, science, the media, and other disci-
plines have received a kind of schizophrenic religion.
They believe in Jesus Christ, but when it comes to areas
like human sexuality, morality, science, law, public policy,
and art, they act and think as if God does not exist.

The reason for this is that they have been indoctri-
nated by a secular educational process, and they have
never really done their intellectual and spiritual home-
work to see if the Bible really is true in every area of life.
Anybody who has ever studied the Bible seriously has
been amazed at how this complex record of God's dealing with mankind from Genesis to Revelation fits together
with an awesome preciseness. The Bible opens up the
dimensions of human nature and psychology like no other
book. While psychology and modern thought go through
cycles and fads, the Bible has been totally consistent with
its accurate portrayal and analysis of the human situation
for centuries.

In addition, the very latest scientific research supports and gives evidence to the biblical viewpoint. Modern physicist Frank J. Tipler, who wrote *The Physics of
Immortality—Modern Cosmology, God and the Resurrection of
the Dead* (New York: Doubleday, 1994), has proved God's
existence through the field of global general relativity,
which is a brand new field of rarefied physics created by
scientists like Stephen Hawking and Roger Penrose. Furthermore, although not a Christian, Michio Kaku, who is
a professor of Theoretical Physics at the City College of
the City University of New York and a Harvard and Berkeley graduate, has written a book entitled *Hyperspace—*

A Scientific Odyssey through Parallel Universes, Time Warps, and the 10th Dimension (New York: Doubleday, 1994). Michio Kaku, who is one of the leading proponents for what is called The Theory of Everything, has helped unlock the deepest secrets of creation. His research looks into what happened before the Big Bang, whether the past can be altered and if gateways to other universes exist. Kaku's theory helps support the idea that a spiritual realm or fourth dimension can exist.

Most of the leaders of our day who belong to the elite classes were taught to believe that the universe consists of only what we can experience with our physical senses. Despite the fact that all the latest research coming out of physics proves that we live in a multidimensional universe, these world leaders are still trapped in the mindset of the 1950s which believed only in materialism.

For the most part, the majority of these leaders in politics, education, science, business, medicine, and other areas have a very limited knowledge of what the Bible actually says. The men who are moving us towards world government have not studied the Book of Revelation, Ezekiel 38 and 39, the Book of Daniel, and Matthew 24 and 25. They do not realize that the Bible predicts a world government and a one-world economic system run by a single leader. These men are operating unconsciously on the philosophical ideas of men who lived a century earlier and who made a conscious decision to reject the Judeo-Christian God and the teachings of the Bible. Men like H.G. Wells, the Fabians, Colonel House, and other planners of a world government constructed their ideas out of a totally humanistic context.

As in the classic story *Frankenstein*, written in 1818 by Mary Shelley, where a scientist creates a monster that goes out of control, so the globalists, elites, and technocrats of our time are going to be horrified when this dream of a one-world utopia becomes the Beast in the Book of Revelation.

Chapter Ten

A Giant Business Deal

When we are talking about the globalist organizations such as the Trilateral Commission, the Council on Foreign Relations, the United Nations, and the Bilderberg Group, it is important that we understand what is really going on. Although I believe these groups do have a specific plan for a new world order and a world government run by a global elite, I believe their primary motive is based on economics. In other words, the coming world government is going to come about primarily for economic reasons and will be the result of a kind of a giant business merger.

The North American Free Trade Agreement (NAFTA) will build the economic foundation that will eventually be transformed into a North American political union in the same way that the European Common Market eventually became the European Economic Community (EEC). It appears that the globe is being divided up into ten different economic regions that will evolve into political regions. The next step will be to unify these ten different regions economically and then politically. Currently, there are over thirty-seven hundred transnational corporations that have combined sales of over $5.5 trillion. These corporations will inevitably affect the political and social structures of our world and help to usher in what has been called the New World Order

I don't think there are a bunch of guys sitting in some smoke-filled room with a giant globe in the background and pentagrams plotting to take control of the planet. Instead, I believe the coming one-world government is more the industrial by-product of multinational corporations like Mitsubishi building big screen televisions in the United States, McDonald's selling hamburgers in Moscow, the Chinese making clothing and toys for American teen-agers, the English company Thompson Electronics buying RCA, and so on. These massive conglomerates are establishing a world market and one-world government which is going to be the end result of giant corporate mergers and acquisitions. Then added to this mix is going to come the social engineers, New Age visionaries, technocrats, and bureaucrats who are going to turn this thing into a global humanistic state where government begins to replace God. Entities like the United States of Europe, GATT (General Agreement on Tariffs and Trade), the United Nations, and the World Trade Organizations are all steps in this direction.

In addition, the management, censorship and control of information by the mass media is not so much a conspiracy as it is the result of the global media being taken over by a small number of corporations who have similar business interests and a common humanistic world view. The interconnectedness of these major media destroys a free media and creates a new kind of corporate media that does not serve the interests of the people but the wishes of the corporations that own them. The result is that you now have a global battle for who controls public opinion and who will control reality in this new world order.

International Trade

My first experience in seeing the global aspect of international trade was when I was in the film business as a producer of feature films. While selling some of the films that I was the executive producer for at the very posh Beverly Wilshire Hotel in Beverly Hills, I remember watching the limousines, Rolls Royces, and Mercedes Benz pull up to the front of the hotel with all the foreign buyers and sellers of movies from around the world. Cigar-smoking movie moguls from around the world would come out of these limos with young starlets hanging on their arms. It was like some kind of international bazaar with everybody speaking a different language, and photographers running all over the place taking publicity photographs. Movie stars would walk through the hallways, and producers and directors would be talking about their latest film deal over cappucino and bottled water.

When we sold the rights to one of our science fiction movies, we would invite foreign distributors to watch a trailer of our film or they could watch the whole picture in a nearby theatre. The movie was then translated into countless languages and shown in theatres and videocassettes around the globe. The Hollywood film industry was one of the first industries to be dependent on revenues from foreign sales. Most pictures produced in Hollywood today would show modest to no profits if they were not sold in foreign markets.

GATT and the World Trade Organization are attempts at creating a set of rules which govern all international trade. They are also an effort at establishing global governance over communications technologies such as telecommunications, television, film, video, laser disc, computers, cable, and satellites. Already, people with access to satellite technology have the capacity to watch news, sports, or movies in Moscow, Japan, Iran, and Mexico from their condo in Westwood, California.

Going Global

We live in a day when multinational corporations have become the prime force in pushing us towards a global society. In the book *Global Reach—The Power of the Multinational Corporations*, Richard J. Barnet and Ronald E. Muller write, "The men who run global corporations are the first in history with the organization, technology, money, and ideology to make a credible try at managing the world as an integrated unit" ([New York: Simon and Schuster, 1974], 13).

The authors cite the fact that Alexander the Great wept by a river bank when he discovered there were no more worlds to conquer. However, he did not actually conquer the whole world because of his ignorance of world geography. The Napoleonic system, the Thousand Year Reich of Adolf Hitler, the massive British Empire, and even the United States have never come close to building a global organization. Barnet and Muller believe that the world cannot be run by military occupation but only through the power of the multinational corporation.

According to a U.S. Department of Commerce report, of 122 U.S.-based multinational corporations, the research revealed that these companies made the majority of their profits overseas. U.S. companies and banks such as Woolworth's, Pfizer, Mobil Oil, Gillette, Coca-Cola, and the First National City Bank earn over 50 percent of their profits overseas. Companies like Pepsi-Cola, McDonald's, Kentucky Fried Chicken, IBM, and Holiday Inn are springing up all over Russia, Europe, and around the world (ibid.).

You can order a Big Mac and large fries from Red Square in Moscow to Peking, China. If you fancy a Pizza Hut pizza after watching an American movie in France, it's no problem. In remote villages in Africa, teen-agers are watching MTV on their satellite receivers. Our world has become, in the words of Marshall McLuhan, a "global village."

Richard J. Barnet and Ronald E. Muller point out, "The managers of global corporations keep telling one another that there can be no integrated world economy without a radical transformation in the 'obsolete' nation state" (Barnet and Muller, *Global Reach*, 20). The globalization of big business has done more to create a one-world society than the United Nations, the World Federalists, and social visionaries combined. Yet, these new corporate globalists recognize that nationalistic sentiments run deep across the globe, and they are seeking to find a positive way of unifying the world, while still finding a positive role for the nation-state. In countries like America, there are still a lot of "red blooded Americans" who still believe in patriotism, the flag, and these people are not just going to go away.

Major corporations like Exxon are trying to cultivate a "world customer," and companies like AT&T are promoting a One World card. The goal of these corporations is to create a kind of "Global Shopping Center" with customers in every nation. Aurelio Pecci, a director of Fiat and organizer of the Club of Rome says, "The global corporation is the most powerful agent for the internationalization of human society" (ibid., 12).

The power of multinational corporations is not new in the world's history. The East India Company conquered a continent and controlled over 250 million people. It had forty-three warships and its own private army. The Virginia Company and the Plymouth Company opened up the entire New World. Throughout history there has always been a close relationship between large companies and their respective nation-states. The interests of the American government and the American corporations are pretty much the same. Now that U.S.-based global corporations have global interests, it is a natural progression that a new global entity or new world order would have to arise to serve these new international interests.

Thomas Jefferson remarked that the loyalty of capitalists is never to any one nation. "Merchants have no country of their own. Wherever they may be they have no ties with the soil. All they are interested in is the source of their profits" (ibid., 77). President Eisenhower made a similar comment when he said, "Capital is a curious thing with perhaps no nationality" (*Global Reach*, 77). Multinational corporations ultimately have no real loyalty to the United States or our Constitution. They are in a quest for ever-expanding profits and, if it is in their best interest to move our nation into some kind of global organization such as GATT or the WTO, then that is what they will do.

Our politicians will never speak out against the wishes of these corporate giants unless they are directly pressured by the voters. However, the majority of the voters can be manipulated and controlled by a mass media that is owned by these same corporations. The large banks and multinational corporations are the prime contributors to political campaigns. Companies like AT&T, American Airlines, Warner-Lambert Pharmaceutical Company, Lehman Corporation (investment banking), Firestone Tire & Rubber Co., Ford Motor Company, Getty Oil, Standard Oil, Phillips Petroleum, IBM, Gulf Oil, Chase Manhattan Bank, Hewlett-Packard, and countless other corporations have made large contributions to political campaigns. Many people would be surprised to discover that some of the same companies and individuals that financed George Bush for president also bankrolled Bill Clinton's campaign. Many of these corporations hedge their bets and seem to be able to further their interests no matter who gets elected.

GATT and the New World Order

GATT, or the General Agreement on Tariffs and Trade, was slipped by the American people shortly after the November elections in 1994. It was the final act of the Uruguay Round of Multilateral Trade Negotiations. It was a twenty-two thousand page and 374 pound document that was not even read by those who signed it. In addition, GATT set up a supersecretive World Trade Organization (WTO) that will administer and enforce global rules of all international business and trade. The World Trade Organization will not be accountable to any government and will be in a sense a world government all of its own.

The first round of GATT was in 1947 in Geneva, Switzerland. After the end of World War II, the United States and Great Britain met to plan a global economic system. This plan included the World Bank, the IMF (International Monetary Fund), and the ITO (International Trade Organization), which was designed to regulate all trade. In 1949 in Annecy, France, the Second Round of Gatt was held to reduce tariffs around the world and pave the way for increased global trading. In 1951 in Torquay, England, the Third Round met; in 1956 GATT held the Fourth Round. During 1960 through 1962 in Geneva, Switzerland, the "Dillon Round" was held to add more countries to GATT. In 1964 through 1967 the "Kennedy Round" was held to create across-the-board tariff reductions. From 1973 through 1979 in Geneva, Switzerland, the "Tokyo Round" met to create a series of special agreements between the nations. Then from 1986 to 1994 in Geneva, Switzerland, the final, or "Uruguay Round," of GATT was held. Negotiations were concluded April of 1994 in Marrakesh, Morocco.

The danger of the GATT treaty is that it is a contractual relationship where the United States has a single vote just like much smaller nations. In addition, Europe will have twelve votes while the United States will only have one vote. Currently, there are 116 member nations in GATT, and anyone of them has the power to shoot down any U.S. proposal. The bottom line is that GATT appears to seriously reduce our national sovereignty, and perhaps this is the plan.

Could it be that there are behind-the-scenes players who are deliberately attempting to redistribute the wealth of industrialized nations like the United States? GATT has powerful critics from unlikely places such as Ross Perot and consumer advocate Ralph Nader. Ralph Nader warned Congress, "These trade agreements are excessively secret. There is no justification for having dispute resolution panels in secret . . . with no requirement that even governments disclose their submissions" (Ralph Nader, "Report on Gatt Pros and Cons," *Congressional Digest* [November 1994], 273). Nader continues to warn us that GATT will surrender the national sovereignty of the United States as well as individual states to the whims of the World Trade Organization without the consent of the American people. Clearly, there is something going on behind the scenes when our politicians deliberately snuck GATT through. In addition, the economic crisis in Mexico should warn us about the dangers of merging our economy with other nations.

It is interesting to observe that the Bible predicted centuries ago that a time would come when all the nations of the earth would be united in some kind of one-world government. This continued push for globalism should be a cause of concern for every Bible-believing Christian. We must remember that the new world order will not be neutral towards Christians or Israel. Christians have values that clearly contradict the beliefs of this global humanistic state, and Israel appears to stand in the way of world peace because it believes that God has given it a right to both Jerusalem and Israel.

The Mexican Bailout

The United Nations has brought about over a dozen U.N.-affiliated trade blocs from regional entities such as the North American Free Trade Agreement (NAFTA), the European Union (EU), and the Asia Pacific Economic Council (APEC). In addition, there exists GATT, the World Trade Organization (WTO), and the Organization for Economic Co-operation and Development. All of these organizations are tied into the United Nations Economic and Social Council.

The Mexican Bailout was an effort by the president of the United States to protect the investments of large Wall Street firms by using the taxpayers money. It was also part of the globalization of the world economy in that the United States and Mexico are connected economically and many American firms are manufacturing products across the border such as automobile manufacturers and Zenith televisions.

The Mexican Bailout was not specifically in the interests of the American people as it was in the interests of Wall Street investment firms and international bankers. The Group of Seven officials from the United States, Canada, France, Britain, Germany, Italy, and Japan expressed "total satisfaction" with President Clinton's $50-billion international aid package for Mexico (Jube Shiver, Jr., "Industrial Nations Support $50 Billion in Mexico Aid," *Los Angeles Times*, Sunday, 5 February 1995, A6).

Nine billion dollars of this bailout came directly out of the U.S. Treasury. This represents two-thirds of our annual foreign aid budget. Interestingly enough, nobody came forward to bail out our own Orange County in California, and it appears U.S. tax dollars were conscripted by our government to bail out Wall Street investors. Our nation is currently sinking before an enormous load of debt, and it is a curious thing that our politicians didn't blink an eye while sending billions to Mexico. The budget of the National Endowment for the Arts is a drop in the bucket compared to this. In fact, the $9 billion figure is fifty times more than the budget for the NAE.

The Mexican Bailout is another example of how our world is rapidly becoming a one-world economy where national economies are directly linked into the global economy and organizations like the International Monetary Fund (IMF).

A Giant Sucking Sound

There is a giant sucking sound in the land. It's the sound of American jobs being sucked south of the border and around the world. Remember, our politicians told us that NAFTA and GATT would help us economically. It was only a few weeks later that American taxpayers had to bail out Mexico to the tune of over $19 billion. You don't have to be a rocket scientist to figure out that you have got to sell an awful lot of products to come up with $19 billion.

If we are not careful, our children are all going to be flipping hamburgers for a living because all of our major industries have gone to Third World countries. Already, the large U.S.-based global firms such as ITT, Ford, Chrysler, Kodak, Procter & Gamble, etc., are employing a large percentage of their work force overseas. It's time for Americans to pressure our elected representatives to develop new manufacturing and high-tech industries here at home before it's too late.

Chapter Eleven

Global Dreams or Global Nightmare?

Paul M. Mazur, who was a partner in the Wall Street investment firm of Lehman Brothers as well as an international economist, issued a clear warning concerning the globalist dreams of some of his powerful business associates. Mazur wrote in his book *Unfinished Business* that as the mechanisms of global interdependence or nations increase in complexity, there would have to be a growing international bureaucracy put in place to control the system. Mazur theorized that this bureaucracy would have to continually grow in scope and authority. According to economist Mazur,

> Finally the large number of governmental bureaus that will have their orbits in the atmosphere cannot be allowed the freedom to compete and collide with one another. So, in order to control the diverse bureaucracies required, a politburo will develop, and over this organization there is likely to arise the final and single arbiter—the master of the order, the total dictator. (Malachi Martin, *The Keys of this Blood—The Struggle for World Dominion Between Pope John Paul II, Mikhail Gorbchev and the Capitalist West* [New York: Simon & Schuster, 1990], 343)

In commenting about Mazur's statement, Malachi Martin, the Jesuit scholar, says,

Certainly everybody would like to dismiss such a
scenario as no more than hyperbole and
speculation. . . . But by the admission of just about
everybody concerned, the good of the nations already depends on what looks very much like a global economy; and Mazur's projection of one form
that global economy could take must be considered
in cold realism. (Ibid., 344)

I believe that this global dream that turned into a
global nightmare is precisely what the Book of Revelation
speaks of in Revelation 13:11–18—the Beast and a one-
world economic system. I think eventually at some point
in the future that this global interdependence and global
governance will be taken over by a person the Bible calls
the Anti-christ.

Freedom from War?

Under the administration of John F. Kennedy, the
Council on Foreign Relations produced a document called
Study Number 7, which helped to create the Department
of State Publication 7277 entitled "Freedom from War—
The United States Program for General and Complete
Disarmament In A Peaceful World." The document called
for the gradual dismantling of U.S. military forces and
the creation of a United Nations army in three stages.
This "Freedom from War" proposal was introduced at
the Sixteenth General Assembly of the United Nations.

This "Freedom from War" document calls for "the
disbanding of all national armed forces and the prohibition of their establishment in any form whatsoever other
than those required to preserve internal order and for
contributions to a United Nations Peace Force." The State
Department publication further states, "As states relin-
quish their arms, the United Nations must be progressively strengthened in order to improve its capacity to
assure international security and the peaceful disarmament of disputes" ("Freedom from War—The United
States Program for General and Complete Disarmament

in a Peaceful World," Department of State Publication 7277, Disarmament Series 5, September 1961, Office of Public Affairs—Bureau of Public Affairs, Washington, D.C., 3, 13).

In addition, the program calls for a Stage III agenda where "no state would have the military power to challenge the progressively strengthened U.N. Peace Force." Basically, what this document proposes is a kind of one-world government ruled by the United Nations. Although, the document calls for a "peaceful world of independent states," which is a noble ambition, one must ask the question just how long the world would be free and peaceful if the wrong man or group took control of the United Nations with no weapons to defend themselves (ibid., 19).

Elliot Abrams, who was an assistant secretary of state under Ronald Reagan dealing with the United Nations, Human Rights and Inter-American Affairs, commented on organizations like the World Federalist Society, the Council on Foreign Relations, and the concept of global government. He suggested that during the Reagan years there was no dismantling of American forces and the strengthening of a U.N. army. However, Abrams believes that Clinton and Secretary Christopher along with others would like to see the role of the United Nations strengthened in terms of world governance.

United Nations Troops on U.S. Soil?

When I first heard that U.N. troops were training on American soil, I thought that it was something made up by some kind of conspiracy nut. Who would have believed it? There are actually United Nations troops training on U.S. soil. According to the *McAlvany Intelligence Advisor* (Phoenix, Arizona, August 1994), United Nations troops and military equipment have been seen in different places throughout the United States such as Myrtle Beach, South Carolina. Plans are also underway for Russian troops to train alongside American troops. There are some reports circulating that the Russian troops are already training in "joint" chemical and biological warfare exercises in the southeastern U.S. and Alaska.

Russian and U.N. military vehicles have been spotted on trains in Montana, Pennsylvania, and Colorado. According to the *McAlvany Intelligence Advisor*, Russian BMP-40 armored cars, which are designed for urban warfare, and Russian UAZ-469B light, jeeplike vehicles were also spotted along with American-built M113 armored personnel carriers, which were painted white with U.N. letters on the side.

Surrendering U.S. Sovereignty to the U.N.

Bill Clinton signed Executive Order, Presidential Decision Directive 13, or what is now designated PDD-25, which was a secret order that placed U.S. forces under the operational control of a foreign commander such as the United Nations. Although the American people were not allowed to see the actual document, the U.S. State Department released a summary of the "Clinton Administration's Policy on Reforming Multilateral Peace Operations." In a nutshell, this directive places U.S. troops under U.N. command in special situations, gives the U.N. privy to U.S. intelligence, repeals the law that limits the amount of troops that the U.S. can commit without congressional approval, and establishes a U.N. peacekeeping fund for U.N. military operations that bypasses Congress.

Pat Buchanan stated, "The Clinton Doctrine as defined by PDD-13 is a surrender of U.S. sovereignty, a betrayal of the ideas upon which our republic was founded" (Donald S. McAlvany, "Moving the U.S. Military Under U.N. Command," *McAlvany Intelligence Advisor* [August 1994], 6).

Why Are We Cutting Defense Spending?

At a recent gathering of the U.S. intelligence community where the heads of the CIA and other intelligence operatives met in Washington, D.C., the term *Hot Peace* was continually thrown about. The term *Hot Peace* refers to our time when the United States is supposedly at peace but the threat from fanaticism and extremism is ever present. This era of Hot Peace is different than the Cold War era we had with the Soviet Union.

Yet, with the threat of terrorism and nuclear war more present today than during the Cold War, the United States is rapidly cutting its defense budget. In 1990 our defense budget was $348.6 billion; in 1992 it was $310.8 billion; in 1994 $266.7 billion; in 1996 it will be $248.8 billion; and by 1999 it will be $237.6 billion (*U.S. News & World Report* [24 October 1994]: 31–33).

In the 1961 State Department publication "Freedom from War: The United States Program for General and Complete Disarmament in a Peaceful World" called for "the disbanding of all national armed forces and the prohibition of their reestablishment in any form whatsoever other than those required to preserve internal order and for contributions to a United Nations Peace force" (p, 11).

Could it be that these cuts in our Defense Department are part of a program designed to reduce the national sovereignty of the United States and make us more reliant on the United Nations for our defense? It sure looks like it. During Operation Desert Shield/Storm, the operation cost around $61.1 billion during 1990 and 1991. The United States paid for about $7.4 billion of the operation (*U.S. News & World Report* [24 October 1994], 31–33). Many military experts believe that if the same crisis arose today we do not have sufficient resources to mount the same level of military operation. Yet, the world is more hostile today then it was then. North Korea has nuclear weapons, and, with the collapse of the Soviet Union, the Soviet nuclear arsenal is leaking into the Middle East.

In central Kaliningrad, on the Baltic, two security guards and a business executive were planning to meet a man from St. Petersburg who was going to sell them nuclear material for $1 million in cash. Fortunately, the police intercepted the operation and grabbed the man who was carrying an eight-inch container holding highly radioactive material and emitting gamma radiation (Bruce W. Nelan, "Formula for Terror," *Time* [29 August 1994], 47).

Unfortunately, these materials from nuclear weapons are being distributed around the world making the term "hot peace" extremely appropriate. In addition, Muslim nations are increasing their military budgets, and our government reacts by cutting our defense budget. It is a strange reaction in a world where some kind of nuclear conflict seems inevitable. Perhaps it can only be explained as part of a game plan to disarm the United States and further establish a new world order.

The real concern over nuclear proliferation is one of the most powerful forces that is fueling the drive for some kind of global government. With the threat of a nuclear strike increasing in the Middle East and with nations like North Korea, the world, in a desperate attempt to establish world peace, is going to agree to some kind of one-world government.

Chapter Twelve

The Commission on Global Governance

At the recent U.N. World Summit for Social Development in Copenhagen, Denmark, a new book was released entitled *Our Global Neighborhood—The Report of the Commission on Global Governance*. Nelson Mandela called the book "a timely work deserving our full attention." The Commission on Global Governance is part of the United Nations effort to transform our world and has the full support of secretary general of the United Nations Boutros Boutros-Ghali.

The commission believes that "global governance is part of the evolution of human efforts to organize life on the planet" and states very clearly that "global governance is not global government" and that "no misunderstanding should arise from the similarity of terms. We are not proposing movement towards world government, for were we to travel in that direction we could find ourselves in an even less democratic world than we have" (*Our Global Neighborhood—The Report of the Commission on Global Governance* [New York: Oxford University Press, 1995], xvi).

It is interesting to note that although the U.N. commission stated that their goal was not world government and that they were concerned about the negative results of global government, in the past the U.N. Development Program's Human Development Report of 1994 used the term *world government*. In an article by Dr. Jan Tinbergen entitled "Global Governance for the 21st Century," Dr.

Tinbergen said, "Mankind's problems can no longer be solved by national governments. . . . What is needed is World Government" (William F. Jasper, "A Plague of Power," *The New American* [1993], 7).

In 1993 Pres. Bill Clinton wrote a letter to the World Federalist Association that was to be read at a banquet honoring the famous author Norman Cousins. Cousins was the man who at one time cured himself of a fatal disease by watching comedy films and taking massive doses of vitamin C. In the letter, President Clinton praised Norman Cousins because he worked for "world government and world peace" (22 June 1993 letter on White House stationery; *The New American* [April 3, 1995], 7, article "A Plague of Power" by William F. Jasper). It is important to note that the president's own words were "world government."

Many years earlier James Paul Warburg, the son of the Council on Foreign Relations founder, Paul Warburg, and a globalist, said to the United States Senate, "We shall have world government whether we like it or not. The only question is whether world government will be achieved by conquest or consent" (Des Griffin, "Descent Into Slavery" [S. Pasadena, CA: Emissary Publications, 1980]: 2, 4).

The Commission on Global Governance goes to great lengths to point out several times in their book that they are not planning "world government" or "world feudalism." Yet, we see that others have often used the words "world government" and even the stronger words of somebody like Warburg. I believe that the majority of people behind the globalist movement are sincere and truly want some kind of utopian world democracy. But, history shows us that the sincere dreams of social visionaries have often been turned into brutal dictatorships by others who lack a conscience and are ruthless.

The problem is that once the creation of a political, economic, and social organism is created to establish world governance, the potential for abuse and a world dictator grabbing the reigns of power is enormous. I believe that the commission is naive regarding human history and human nature when it comes to building any kind of centralized bureaucracy to run any nation or the world. However, I think that the Commission on Global Governance and the U.N. believe that what they are doing is in the best interests of mankind. In reality, though, they may be unwittingly setting the stage for an oppressive world government and the emergence of a world dictator.

Global Pressure

Pop singer Billy Joel wrote a song called "Pressure." In the song Joel describes the pressures of modern life that can drive a person crazy. Our world is in a time of great social upheaval, which creates enormous political and sociological pressure. The late Dr. Francis Schaeffer wrote about the effects of such pressures in his classic work *How Should We Then Live?* In the book, Schaeffer talks about the ancient Roman bridges that were built over the many streams of Europe and how these bridges were built for people and wagons to cross over. Yet, centuries later when heavily loaded trucks would attempt to cross over them they would collapse because they could not stand the pressure that these modern vehicles placed on their structures.

Francis Schaeffer used this analogy to talk about how fragile our culture and freedoms are in modern society. Today, many of the democratic social and political structures were built for a world that did not have high technology and global unrest. As a result, there is enormous pressure on our political institutions to handle pressures that they were not designed to handle. The growth to the United Nations and the move towards global governance is partially the result of mankind's attempts to solve the increased pressures of a high-tech global society that has become economically and socially interdependent.

The Commission on Global Governance is a response to the crime, drug abuse, high unemployment, urban stress, racial tensions, proliferation of nuclear weapons,

terrorism, disease, and famines that have spread throughout the whole earth. The problem is that the pressures
increase the need for some kind of authoritarian political
structure of a global scale. In response to these global
pressures, the United Nations has had to expand its role
in the peacekeeping operations that it began in 1948.
The United Nations currently has peacekeeping forces,
and many of those are American soldiers, in the following
nations: Israel, Syria, India, Pakistan, Egypt, Lebanon,
Congo, West New Guinea, Yemen, Cyprus, Iran, Iraq,
Nambia, Angola, El Salvador, Kuwait, former Yugoslavia,
Mozambique, Somalia, Cambodia, Haiti, Liberia, Georgia, Uganda, Rwanda, and other locations.

During 1994 the United Nations had over seventy
thousand soldiers deployed around the world at a cost of
around $5 billion. With the threat of North Korean nuclear
missile sites and the fact that some scientists from the
Soviet Union are prepared to sell nuclear technology and
weapons to nations like Iran, the stakes in the global
game have raised considerably.

We, the Peoples?

One of the most important statements in the Constitution of the United States is the phrase, "We the people."
The idea is that our elected form of government represents the will of the people. Many people are going to be
in for a shock when they begin to hear the phrase, "We,
the peoples" in reference to the United Nations. Like it
or not, we are on the verge of a global transformation
that will create citizens of the planet rather than citizens
of the United States. This change in consciousness is one
of the purposes of Earth Day, which is an attempt to get
us to think of ourselves as citizens of Spaceship Earth.

When the United Nations was established on 24 October 1945, it had the following goals:

- to practice tolerance and live together in peace with
  one another as good neighbors;

- to unite our strength to maintain international peace and security;
- to ensure, by the acceptance of principles and the institution of methods, that armed force shall not be used, save in the common interest; and
- to employ international machinery for the promotion of the economic and social advancement for all peoples (*Our Global Neighborhood*, 231).

Clearly, at first glance, these goals seem harmless. Yet, if the United Nations exists for "We, the peoples," then why are we not being told of all of its plans? Why are there not open and free elections? And, why is the whole United Nations agenda being concealed? In addition, recent history has shown us the dangers of governmental institutions that were for the "people." Communist Russia, Communist China, and Cuba were all supposedly for the "people." However, they were not free and ended up horribly oppressing the people.

I Pledge Allegiance to the Flag of the United States of Earth

Picture the classroom of the future where a group of fourth graders begin their day by reciting these words, "I pledge allegiance to the flag of the United States of Earth, one world indivisible." Instead of the American flag, there will be a brand new flag with a picture of planet earth on it. Instead of pictures of Abraham Lincoln and George Washington, there will be pictures of Nelson Mandela, Boutros Boutros-Ghali; and, instead of Betsy Ross, there will be picture of Margaret Sanger, the founder of Planned Parenthood.

Does that sound all that far-fetched? I don't think so. This multicutural, diversity training, politically correct revolution is leading right to that kind of future. In most classrooms in the United States, they don't even say the Pledge of Allegiance anymore. They are trained not to be U.S. citizens but citizens of the world.

International Law and the World Court

In the future we may not see anymore Judge Wopners or Judge Itos holding court. In fact, our entire system of courts and laws may one day be replaced by some kind of world court and international law. Our judges would be appointed by the United Nations, and, instead of an American flag hanging in the court, there would be a giant picture of planet earth in the center of the courtroom.

In *Our Global Neighborhood—The Report of the Commission on Global Governance*, the authors state, "In an ideal world, acceptance of compulsory jurisdiction of the World Court would be a prerequisite for U.N. membership" (ibid., 308). The idea is that the rule of International Law established by the U.N. and the World Court run by the U.N. would become the highest law of planet earth. The problem that arises is, who would appoint these judges and on what basis would they make their decisions.

One of the goals of the United Nations is to strengthen the International Law and the World Court. This is why the United States signed the U.N. Conference on the Rights of the Child. It was signed because it is a kind of treaty that will have legal bearing in the future. The problem with this International Law and the World Court is that it circumvents our Constitution and Bill of Rights, which protect our human and religious freedoms. However, there is no guarantee that International Law and a World Court would do the same. Our nation was originally founded as "one nation under God," and now there are plans to replace this with "one world under man." The difference will be that America was built on Judeo-Christian principles, and the United Nations is built solely on humanistic principles.

Lessons from History

We are on the verge of major social change—a revolution, if you will, in the way our world will be governed. The United Nations and the coming of some kind of world governance is going to be as significant as any of the major revolutions in history. As such, it is important to learn the historical lessons from previous revolutions in history. In *How Should We Then Live?*, Dr. Francis Schaeffer explains that every major societal change and revolution is based on some kind of philosophical foundation or premise (*How Should We Then Live?* reprinted in the *Complete Works of Francis A. Schaeffer*, vol. 5 [Crossway Books: 1982]).

The Bloodless Revolution of England in 1688 made the English Parliament an equal partner to the Crown. This was a bloodless revolution because it was based on many of the Christian principles of the Reformation and brought more freedom into English life. In distinct contrast, the French Revolution was based on the humanistic philosophy of men like Voltaire (1694–1778) and the so-called Enlightenment, which rejected the teachings of the Bible in favor of man's ideas. The result of this humanistic revolution was a bloodbath and the coming of an authoritarian ruler, Napoleon Bonaparte, to restore order.

Interestingly enough, in Voltaire's home in Fernery, France, there was a large painting of the goddess Diana with a crescent moon on her head and one under her feet, reaching down to help mankind. Voltaire had rejected the true God of the Bible in favor of Diana and a goddess of reason. Consequently, the French Revolution, which began with noble ideas and high hopes, ended in the Reign of Terror.

In contrast, the American Revolution of 1776 led to freedom, democracy, and the Bill of Rights because it was birthed in biblical principles and a clear Judeo-Christian world view. It was precisely because of the Judeo-Christian philosophical base of our Founding Fathers that our nation has been the freest and most productive on earth.

The Russian Revolution, which was based on the humanistic ideas of Karl Marx, ended up like the French Revolution, with Lenin becoming an authoritarian dictator. The philosophical ideas of Karl Marx (1818–1883) and his *Manifesto of the Communist Party* brought about the murder of millions of people, authoritarian government, and totalitarianism.

Dr. Francis Schaeffer, who spent a lifetime analyzing these events, taught that ideas have consequences and that the philosophy behind great social movements and revolutions will determine their outcome. The reason this global revolution, or move to world governance, is so dangerous is that it ignores the clear lessons of history. A massive system is being put into place with laws, courts, and a military and economic system with a humanistic philosophical base. Despite how optimistic and well intended the architects are of this new world order, the end result will be betrayal, tyranny, totalitarianism, and the darkest period the world has ever known.

The reason for this is that the globalist society that is being constructed is being built purely on humanistic principles that are without the checks and balances of a Christian world view. The reason the American form of government has been so effective is because it had a biblical world view. It recognized that man is sinful and in need of a Savior. As a result, checks and balances were put into our governmental system: different branches of government holding one another accountable, a Constitution, and the power of the people to elect their representatives.

This coming world government has no such checks and balances. It is built on the myth that man is basically good and evolving into higher consciousness. This was the same kind of myth that seduced the leaders of the Enlightenment when they paraded the goddess of reason through the streets of France. And, it was a similar myth that seduced the Marxist revolutionaries. The world government is going to be betrayed, hijacked, and eventually taken over by some kind of authoritarian elite. The Bible teaches us that someday in the future a supernatural dictator is going to arise and seize control of this world government. Perhaps he is simply waiting for its systems to be put in place.

Chapter Thirteen

The New World Order and Family Values?

There has been a lot of press lately about family values. However, most of the public discussion has not been open and honest. Instead, a very powerful organization has been using its influence behind the scenes to promote its own agenda regarding family values. The Rockefeller Brothers Fund, which was worth about $242,120,725, has been investing millions in grants which, among other things, "support efforts in the U.S. and abroad that contribute ideas, develop leaders, and encourage institutions in the transition to global interdependence" (Pat Robertson, *The New World Order* [Dallas, TX: Word Publishing, 1991], 139).

It is obvious that the Rockefeller Brother's Fund is spending its considerable fortune to promote global government. However, it does not stop there. According to the Rockefeller Brother's Fund own book entitled *The Unfinished Agenda*, they also plan to do the following:

- Establish a national goal of population stabilization or gradual population decrease, with small family as a desirable and socially responsible ideal.
- Increase support for family planning organizations and provide aid for clinics that offer contraceptives, pregnancy testing, abortion, and sterilization.
- Provide positive publicity to women in positions of responsibility, and to the creative possibilities open to those with small families.

- Establish sex and family education programs for pre-teens and teen-agers.
- Provide positive publicity for those who have chosen not to marry or to have children.

In addition, *The Unfinished Agenda* calls for tax plans that favor singles, the unmarried, and people with small families (*The Unfinished Agenda: The Citizens Policy Guide to Environmental Issues;* A Task Force Report sponsored by the Rockefeller Brother's Fund, Crowell, editor, Gerald O. Barney, 1977, New York, 12, 29, and 30).

It is quite shocking to think that the public debate over traditional family values has been honest and open, only to discover that the debate has been shaped by a powerful organization that is attempting to promote its own values. Is it any wonder that millions of people have chosen to live together in our nation, have abortions, and, if they do marry, have hardly any children? The national media has been promoting these values, and even our tax codes favor this lifestyle. If our media was truly objective and honest, there would have been news stories that gave full disclosure to what organizations like the Rockefeller Brothers Fund is attempting to do. They have every right to promote their own agenda, but what is alarming is the fact that this agenda is often hidden and our news media does not report important facts regarding these issues.

The Global Population Agenda

During the International Conference on Population Development (ICDP) in Cairo, members from over 184 nations met to map out a twenty-year plan to reduce the world's population. International Planned Parenthood (IPP) led the 1994 population conference. The Cairo conference promoted the idea that the world is overpopulated and that many of the world's problems are due to population growth.

Vice Pres. Al Gore was a key spokesperson at the United Nations Cairo conference, which met to "stabi-

lize" the world's population. One of the biggest critics of
the conference was the Vatican. Monsignor Peter Elliot,
who was a member of the Vatican's delegation to Cairo,
said of the U.N. conference, "This could be described as
the largest Planned Parenthood meeting in history"
("Planned Parenthood's Global Agenda," *CBN World
Watch—A Report on Events With A Biblical Viewpoint*, vol. 2,
no. 1 [January/February 1995]: 1).

The History of Population Control

The modern population control movement can be
traced back to Thomas Malthus, who wrote his "Essay on
the Principle of Population" in 1878, which taught that
many of the world's problems are due to excessive population growth. Charles Darwin was influenced by Malthus
when he developed his theories on natural selection. And,
Margaret Sanger (1888–1966) who founded Planned Parenthood, believed that birth control and abortion were
the solution to the world's population problems.

Population control has become one of the goals of the
globalist movement, and it is no accident that here in the
United States there are many powerful players in what is
called the prochoice movement. When people who are
prolife stand up and legitimately protest abortion, they
are coming up against not only feminists and abortion-
ists, they are in conflict with a powerful globalist establishment that has enormous influence over the mass media,
the courts, and the political system.

In Genesis 1:28, God makes a statement that is pro-
foundly different from Thomas Malthus and the United
Nations. God said, "Be fruitful and multiply; fill the earth
and subdue it." In Genesis 9:7 God also says, "And as for
you be fruitful and multiply; bring forth abundantly in
the earth and multiply in it." And, Psalm 127:3 states,
"Behold, children are a heritage from the Lord, the fruit
of the womb is a reward."

What is really happening here is that there is a conflict between the commands of God and the agenda of

man. The globalist elite have decided in their human wisdom that it is not good for man to "be fruitful and multiply." As a result, they are using their considerable influence to promote abortion, family planning, and living together instead of marriage. The tragedy is that millions of people are going to be cheated out of the joys of marriage and having children. This is no small thing.

As someone who formerly bought into this not-having-children mentality, my wife and I were married for over fifteen years before we had any children. Now, we have three lovely children, and it is one of the most awesome blessings a person can have. There are no words to describe the rich fulfillment that having children can bring. The positive effects to society that a loving family can contribute are countless in terms of the reduction of crime, the increase of personal happiness, and economic stabilization. Yet, here we have powerful forces in the new world order doing everything they can to undermine this God-given principle.

Meet the New Family

The traditional family is under attack, and the social engineers have been working overtime to design a new model. The new model of the family will consist of homosexual partners raising children, people living together, and an entire range of blended families. It is already increasingly common for single women to have a man purposely get them pregnant so that they can a have a child.

It is true that God is in the redemption business, and He will reach out and restore single mothers, the divorced, and any number of relationships because He loves people. But, God's original model for the family is that a man and woman marry each other for life and stay committed to each other.

Not only have we come a long way from the days of Ozzie and Harriet, Dick van Dyke and the "Leave It to Beaver" families, we have actually turned a corner where dysfunctional families like the ones portrayed in "Married with Children" and "The Simpsons," and the two troubled teen-agers in "Beavis and Butthead" are now the subject of our humor. But, underneath all the empty laughter are lots of shattered lives, a suicide rate among teenagers that is at an all-time high, and people who are lonely, hurting, and in pain. In addition, the widespread acceptance of homosexuality with major sports, entertainment and media figures coming "out of the closet" has contributed to the antifamily lifestyles. When rock legend Elton John and the publisher of *Rolling Stone* magazine Jan Wenner openly boast of their gay lifestyles, these people become role models for young people who seek to emulate their lives.

God designed the family to be a healing center for people where they can be loved, accepted, and protected from the world. With the family under assault, one of the main centers of psychological support has been taken away, and the result is social chaos. Furthermore, the widespread use of pornography, relaxed sexual values, the increase of working mothers along with the reliance on daycare, men who sacrifice their families on the altars of their careers, and the tendency of people to opt for easy divorce rather than working their problems out, have all contributed to the destruction of the family.

The U.N. Convention on the Rights of the Child

There are some very powerful people in this world who want to take away your right to raise your children the way you see fit. With the backing of Hillary Clinton and over fifty U.S. senators, there is an attempt being made to ratify the United Nations Convention on the Rights of the Child, which has already become the law of the land in over 150 nations and is designed to empower the United Nations to dictate to you how you can raise your children.

In 1988 an agreement was reached by children's rights activists to create a panel of so-called experts appointed

by the United Nations to give children certain "rights."
At first glance, this sounds like a noble idea. However,
when you dig deeper you discover that these so-called
children's rights include giving children the right to reject their parents' authority, morals, values, and religious
upbringing.

The U.N. Convention on the Rights of the Child is
being sent to the Senate under the title of S.R. 70, or
Senate Resolution 70, and has the support of the National Education Association (NEA), the National Council
of Churches, the Children's Defense Fund (where Hillary
Clinton worked as the fund's legal counsel), Planned Parenthood, American Bar Association, the Girl Scouts of
America, and other groups. Although the convention does
provide valuable protection for children in underdevel-
oped nations, the provision is excessive and unnecessary
in democratic nations like the United States. If passed,
the convention will transfer parental authority to the state
and the United Nations.

In a nutshell, the bill would totally undermine Christian parents' right to raise their children according to
God's standards and force them to indoctrinate their
children with politically correct and humanistic values
and beliefs. Here are just a few of the things that the
convention would do:

Article Three empowers the state and not the parents
to pursue the "best interest of the child."

Article Four gives government bureaucrats the right
to regulate families according to United Nations dictates.

Article Seven forces parents to register their children
with the government.

In Article Thirteen parents would be forced to allow
their children to have full exposure to all kinds of pornography, rock 'n' roll music, films, and television and
could not stop the child from viewing or listening to this
material under the guise of freedom of expression.

Article Fourteen gives children the legal right to refuse
to go to church or receive religious training.

Article Nineteen creates a massive government bureaucracy that would check up on parents and make sure these "rights" were enforced.

Article Twenty-eight creates a compulsory education system that would indoctrinate children with politically correct educational programs that would conflict with parents' desire to raise their children according to the Bible.

And, Article Twenty-nine gives the state the authority to regulate the education and upbringing of the child in accordance with the philosophy of the United Nations, which is based on humanistic ideas.

Commenting on the treaty, the Family Issues Alert bulletin from the Public Policy Division of Focus on the Family states, "Proponents of the treaty have launched an aggressive campaign to make it appear family-friendly, but the treaty clearly promotes global intrusion into family sovereignty. Its effect will be perilous if passed" (Focus on the Family, *Family Issues Alert* [16 February 1995]: 1).

Whoever Rocks the Cradle Rules the World

In the Illinois General Assembly in 1994, there was a move called Parenting Program SB159, which was a forty-seven-page program that would have given the government the power to invade people's private homes and send government employees inside the home to supervise what is going on. This bill would have given the Illinois public school system the authority to supervise all children beginning at the time of their birth. It is another example of how a hidden elite is attempting to take control over our children, and, as Phyllis Schlafly said, "Whoever rocks the cradle rules the world. . . . Powerful groups are lined up to empower the government, rather than parents to rock the cradle" (Phyllis Schlafly, "Should Schools Be Parents of Preschoolers?" *Christian American* [February 1994]: 2).

OBE and Goals 2000

Both Houses of Congress passed the Goals 2000: Educate America Act, which is a $240 million education reform proposal that will have far-reaching affects on the way your children are being educated. One of the things this act will do is fund what is called OBE, or Outcome Based Education, and an early "childhood intervention program." This childhood intervention program will allow "surrogate parents" trained by the government to visit families and make sure they are complying to government standards on child rearing. Sen. Tom Harkin (D-IA) said before Congress that he thoroughly agreed with the report, which stated, "We must rethink education in America. Education begins at birth and preparation for education begins before birth. Let us get these kids right after birth" (Connie Zhu, "You Just Lost More Freedom," *Christian American* [April 1994]: 6).

Beverly Lahaye of Concerned Women for America says that Goals 2000 will fund school sex clinics, teen-age abortions, psychologists for very young children, government parent reeducation programs, and multicultural programs. OBE will also teach students to be open to other sexual lifestyles with its "Multicultural and Worldview; and Open Mind to Alternative Perspectives." OBE will not emphasize academics like reading, writing, and arithmetic. Rather, it will stress "attitudes" instead of academics. A student who does not accept the ideas in "An Open Mind to Alternative Perspectives" may be held back from graduating (ibid., 6).

A License in Order to Have Children?

There is a serious discussion going on in our society now about possibly making it mandatory for parents to receive a state license before they can have children. One of the proposals requires American parents to get a state license before they can raise children. These licenses would be checked in hospital maternity wards and unlicensed parents could lose their children permanently.

It sounds like something you would read about in Russia or Communist China. Yet, this plan is being seriously considered by psychologists and other authorities. There are those people in our society who would like the state to raise your children so that they can indoctrinate them with their humanistic value system. The U.N. Convention on the Rights of the Child and this current debate about licensing parents are all moving us in the direction of the state attempting to raise our children.

Former Prime Minister Margaret Thatcher used the term "Nanny State" to describe big government's attempt to control every facet of our society including child rearing. Government has no business being a nanny or a parent. Families have been around since the beginning of time, and there is no substitute for a real mother and father raising their children with godly values (Marshall Wittman, "Just Say No to the Nanny State," *Christian American* [March 1994], 21).

Chapter Fourteen

The Fallout from Oklahoma City

All law-abiding Americans support our government's efforts to uncover terrorist acts before they happen. Perhaps, if the FBI had not been underfunded to begin with, they could have prevented the Oklahoma City tragedy before it happened. Clearly, the FBI and other governmental agencies need the funds and manpower necessary to stop terrorist activities from abroad and at home. I wholeheartedly support the efforts of our government to legitimately "beef up" counter-terrorist activities.

However, there is always a danger if we proceed without prudence and common sense in these areas. After a meeting to increase the government's power to pursue terrorists, Bob Dole said, "We need to be very careful in how we proceed. . . . There are certain areas involving people's rights that we have to go very slowly on." One of the proposed elements of the counter-terrorism law would include "relaxing current restrictions on military involvement in the criminal investigations of civilians so that investigators can tap military expertise in terrorism involving biological or chemical weapons" and "giving wider discretion to use court-approved warrants on wiretapping and other surveillance, including proposals to make it easier to monitor cellular phones" (Michael Ross, "Clinton Unveils Proposals to Counter Terrorist Acts," *Los Angeles Times*, 27 April 1995, 17).

During the Senate Judiciary Committee on Terrorism in the U.S. on 27 April 1995, Sen. Alan Simpson raised the question, would a digitized national I.D. card be helpful in keeping terrorism out of the United States? Clearly, our government officials are investigating the possibilities of using the new technology to deter terrorism in our nation.

During the 1960s, the FBI monitored the activities of civil rights groups and Vietnam War protesters on the vague grounds that they were part of a massive anti-American conspiracy. However, there is a real potential for abuse of these powers. Dr. Francis Schaeffer warned that when a society begins to breakdown through random violence and terrorism, some kind of authoritarian government will eventually emerge. Schaeffer said, "There are only two roads to the same end. There is no difference between an authoritarian government from the right or the left: the results are the same. An elite, an authoritarianism as such, will gradually force form on society so that it will not go on to chaos. And most people will accept it—from the desire for personal peace and affluence . . . That is just what Rome did with Caesar Augustus" (Francis Schaeffer, *How Should We Then Live*, *Complete Works of Francis Schaeffer*, vol. 5 [Westchester, Illinois: Crossway Books, 1982], 244).

This kind of authoritarian government is not likely to emerge overnight. However, as the social chaos continues to escalate, and terrorism, violence, and lawlessness increases, the government will have to increase its power in order to keep society from falling apart. This is what we are seeing now. Something has to be done to protect the American people from terrorism, violence, and crime.

The Spin Doctors

A new expression has been coined in our day of global electronic news and that is the idea of the "Spin Doctor." The Spin Doctor is a news journalist or reporter who takes a news story and puts a slant on it so that it says what he or she wants it to say. The Spin Doctors were hard at work right after the Oklahoma tragedy. The major news media continually used the term *right wing extremist* to describe the madmen who bombed the federal building in Oklahoma City. Interestingly, the media also uses the term *right wing extremists* to apply to Newt Gingrich and the Republicans who won their offices in the 1994 election. *Right wing extremist* is regularly used to describe Americans who call themselves Christians and go to church or anybody who is prolife. Men like Pat Robertson and Dr. James Dobson and countless other Christian and conservative leaders are called right wing extremists. It is really outrageous to paint with such a broad brush that you place conservatives and Christians in the same camp as the murderers who bombed the federal building.

Time magazine did a cover story entitled "How Dangerous Are They?—An Inside Look at America's Antigovernment Zealots." In the article, *Time* stated,

> The ranks of the antifederalist insurgency include plenty of the former: tax protesters, home schoolers, Christian fundamentalists and well-versed constitutionalists. But the groups also contain an insidious sprinkling of the latter, including neo-Nazi's and white supremacists. What binds these groups together is fervent paranoia. (Jill Smolowe, "Enemies of the State," *Time* [8 May 1995]: 62)

Time magazine is putting Bible-believing Christians and homeschoolers in the same group as Nazis and white supremacists. This is outrageous! During the same week, *Newsweek* and *U.S. News & World Report* ran similar cover stories. *New York Magazine*; in May, 1995, had a cover story that boldly read "UN-AMERICANS," with unflattering pictures of Rush Limbaugh, Oliver North, Jesse Helms, Gordon Liddy, and Pat Robertson. The article accused these men of helping to cause the Oklahoma City bombing.

It's like we are living in the former Soviet Union or in George Orwell's dictatorship in his novel *1984*, where the "Thought Police" would arrest you if you were guilty of "thought crimes" against the state. What we are seeing is certain parts of our government acting in collusion with the media in an attempt to "brainwash" the American public. This is exactly how the hatred of the Jews began in Nazi Germany when Hitler would print material and produce films that caused the people to begin to despise the Jews.

People who see the coming one-world government and the new world order as biblical signs of the last days are being labeled "right-wing extremists" and "paranoid." This is a form of psychological coercion deliberately designed to silence all those who oppose world government and the new world order. The mass media in our society often use psychological manipulation through images, sound bites, spin, and editing in an attempt to lead the masses in a particular direction. Since many people in our society do not read or think for themselves, they are easily swayed by these techniques. In recent years, Bible-believing Christians and conservatives have been the target of attacks from the mass media. There have been consistent news stories that have been designed to "demonize" and "ghettoize" Christians and those who support prayer in schools, those who are prolife, and who support family values.

Right after the Oklahoma City bombing, there were numerous stories on television and the press about "paranoid delusions," "paranoia," and radical fringe groups. The idea was to place anybody who is suspicious about certain government activities, the United Nations, and related subjects as having paranoid delusions. This is a powerful form of psychological manipulation.

In the Soviet Union, people who resisted the Communist party or who disagreed with its goals were put into psychiatric hospitals and mental wards to be "reconditioned" and shot up with drugs. Anybody who did not go along with the Communist party was declared "mentally ill" and lost their civil rights. Make no mistake about it; the psychological manipulation of the mass media and the political correctness movement are all steps in this direction. They are designed to pressure people to conform to a particular humanist world view. It is a form of manipulation. It is equally manipulative to suggest that "Talk Radio" was responsible for the bombing. It seems that there are some in our society that would like to censor free speech, stop dissent, and silence all criticism of the government. But, this is what makes America great. The fact that we can express our opinions openly and that there is a democratic process is what makes America different than Russia, China, Cuba, Iran, and other nations where there is no freedom.

If this trend continues unchecked we are going to see more and more of our freedoms taken away by the government. Already, because there have been fanatics and madmen who have murdered abortion doctors, this has been used as an excuse to take away the civil rights of those who wish to peacefully protest in front of an abortion clinic. The media has used these few isolated incidents to generate hatred and suspicion of those who call themselves prolife.

In Los Angeles, there was a meeting of "Promise Keepers" where over seventy thousand men jammed a sports stadium and stood up for family values and confessed the sin of racism. It was like there was a news black-out on the event or as if it never happened because the media ignored it. If there had been five homosexual activists, this would have been front-page news.

There are dangerous trends in our society that are preparing the way for a time when Christians will be violently persecuted, and at some time in the future the Anti-christ will emerge.

Paranoid or Realism?

In what was called the famous "Twinkie Defense," a team of lawyers claimed that eating too many Hostess Twinkies caused their client to go crazy because all the sugar made him paranoid and crazy. Charles Manson and his followers claimed they heard secret messages about revolution while listening to the Beatle's *White Album*. In the old classic movie *The Manchurian Candidate*, actor Frank Sinatra plays a soldier who is brainwashed by the North Koreans to assassinate the president. These are all examples of what psychologists call "paranoid delusions."

However, there is a difference between paranoia, suspicion, and just plain old healthy skepticism. When Oliver Stone directed his Academy Award-winning movie *JFK*, he was accused by the press of being paranoid. But, Stone was just putting his suspicions about the Kennedy assassination on the movie screen. If you wanted to you could accuse best-selling author Michael Cricton of *Jurassic Park* and *Congo* fame of being paranoid when at a gathering of journalists he criticized the major media for trying to control the flow of information.

In the following chapters on Big Brother-type technology, I am not trying to cultivate an attitude of paranoia. I am simply outlining the possibilities that some of the new technology will bring, as well as showing its potential for abuse. Technology is neither good nor evil, but placed in the wrong hands it could be a tool for oppression.

It is not too far-fetched to think that the Anti-christ could eventually use this new technology to control entire populations in what the Book of Revelation calls the mark of the Beast (Rev. 14:11). The mark of the Beast, or 666, is going to be stamped on the forehead or hand of everyone who chooses to worship the Anti-christ. This could be a laser imprint, or what is called biometric technology.

Our society is changing rapidly. Many of us still remember the time when you went to the supermarket and paid by cash. Now people pay by checks or credit cards with laser scanners. Soon all business transactions will be electronic, and it doesn't take much imagination to see the day when even credit cards will be obsolete. Banks understand that credit cards can be stolen. Many businesses are beginning to keep electronic signatures on file in order to prevent theft. The next step will be to get rid of credit cards and give everyone a microchip buried under their skin that can be accessed through laser technology. This could be the mark of the Beast.

Chapter Fifteen

Big Brother Is Watching You

The average person has no idea how much of their life can be monitored through technology and who is monitoring them and for what purpose. Imagine a typical day for an ordinary person. He gets up at 7:00 A.M. and turns on a local television news channel and eats breakfast. Then, he gets dressed and gets in his car in order to drive to work in a nearby city. On the way to work, he stops at a gas station and uses a credit card to buy gas, a cup of coffee, and a newspaper.

What the person does not realize is that every single one of these activities can be tracked from a central location using a computer. There is an electronic device on the market that can even track what television station you are watching. Using bar codes and your credit card number, they can determine what kind of clothes you purchased right down to the size and color. They know how many miles you drive to work each day by tracking the price of your gasoline consumption. The bar codes and entries of the coffee you purchased can tell them whether or not you drink regular or decaf and which paper you read.

In a *New York Times* article (3 May 1995) entitled "The Road Watches You," writer Simon Garfinkle reported that highway authorities around the nation are building "smart-road systems" that will unclog traffic jams and improve driver safety. But, Garfinkle warns that this is just the beginning of a nationwide plan of intelligent transportation systems that can be used by the government to monitor millions of drivers. This data can be stored in a centralized computer bank, allowing the government to watch where you drive everyday.

In fact, all kinds of information about your life can be tracked. When you go shopping at the supermarket, they keep an electronic record of what kinds of items you purchased, which they can use for marketing purposes. However, by analyzing your shopping habits, all kinds of things can be determined about you. And, if you contribute to nonprofit organizations and are on the mailing lists of certain groups, a government bureaucrat can determine your political beliefs. Furthermore, if you walk into most retail stores, banks, shopping malls, and many kinds of businesses, there are television cameras silently being aimed at you. It all sounds a lot like George Orwell's terrifying novel *1984*, where Big Brother watched your every move.

In reality, with the advent of new technologies, the government's, as well as anybody's, capacity to track your life has grown immensely. In fact, all kinds of information about you is being sold on the open market, including credit reports, who you might donate money to, and what kind of magazines you read. Why do you think you keep receiving all kinds of new junk mail, credit card offers, and the like? People are buying and selling information about you all the time without your knowing it.

Big Brother Is Listening to You

Have you ever thought your phone was being tapped because you heard strange clicks or other noises? Well, the whole idea of tapping a person's phone with electronic clips and a tape recorder is almost prehistoric. Now through a new technology called "automated voice recognition," it is possible for a computer to listen to millions of phone calls at once and recognize certain people as well as specific words, phrases, or terms (Charles

Ostman, "Total Surveillance: Your Life on a Chip," *Mondo 2000* [Winter 1995], 20). For example, in a few years when the telephone companies introduce Asynchronous Transfer Mode (ATM), all communications will be directed through a universal communication channel, which will make electronic eavesdropping much easier. A company like Dialogic Corporation located in New Jersey is creating a special automated speech recognition system.

These and other technologies could be used to search through millions of telephone conversations. For example, if the CIA was looking for a terrorist, they could monitor a million phone calls in New York City while a computer searched for key words such as *bomb*, *explosive*, etc. This whole process would have been impossible to do a few years ago, but now a computer can sift through millions of phone calls searching for key words or phrases.

Can you imagine under the global government of the Anti-christ how a computer could listen to millions of phone calls searching for words like *born-again*, *Jesus Christ*, *Bible*, or *washed in the blood*?

Total Surveillance

Technology is rapidly changing our world. In the near future, every American citizen will have some kind of national ID card imbedded with computer information and a personal file. In Chantily, Virginia, a one-million-square-foot complex for the National Reconnaissance Organization is being completed. Its purpose is to develop and manage all U.S. reconnaissance satellites. However, the NRO is also involved in such technologies as ultrahigh storage capacity holographic films that allow huge amounts of personal information to be stored on a national ID card. Interestingly, the NRO has the largest budget of any U.S. intelligence agency (ibid., 16).

In Europe, there is a new giant computer system that connects almost one thousand of the world's largest banks and transfers over $5 trillion every single day. It has been said that these computers have been set up to give every person alive a special eighteen digit number, which records your age, sex, birth date, social security number, and street address, for the coming cashless society. Using the kind of satellite technology employed by the National Reconnaissance Organization, a global street map has been generated by computer.

In fact, satellite technology has advanced to such a high degree that the French-owned company SPOT Image of Reston, Virginia, can sell up-close satellite transmissions of you having a barbecue in your backyard. These surveillance satellites are so powerful that while revolving the earth in outer space they can determine whether you are cooking chicken or steak on the grill. Another company called World Map has spy satellites that can zero in even closer. Approximately thirty countries including Israel, Germany, and China are planning to launch satellite surveillance systems.

TRW, which is the same company that maintains and sells detailed credit reports about you, is also involved in this new $8 billion market. In the movie *Clear and Present Danger*, which was based on the novel by Tom Clancy, actor Harrison Ford is tracked all around the world through special government spy satellites. When he is down in South America hunting down drug dealers, cellular phone calls, television programs, and everything else that is being broadcast were being monitored by intelligence agencies in an effort to catch the criminals.

In fact, a brand new surveillance technology is available which can monitor from over a mile away what is being typed into your computer. Clearly, the potential for abuse of these technologies is staggering, and the capacity to control entire populations through computer technology is also staggering.

Smart Cameras

Not only are powerful cameras being placed in orbital satellites for surveillance, but there is a whole new generation of video cameras on the market that can literally think for themselves with computer technology. These new security cameras are intelligent cameras that have been programmed to recognize what a trained security specialist looks for. Using artificial intelligence, they look for certain body motions, clothing, faces, eye movements, and specific people.

The newest wave of intelligent cameras will operate with "content addressable imagery," which means they can automatically detect the content of sophisticated images, such as facial characteristics, and match it up against a photograph. In the city of Los Angeles, there was a proposal to place surveillance cameras in certain high-crime areas. Through the use of intelligent cameras and the photographs of certain drug dealers and criminals, these cameras could instantly recognize criminals or those engaged in illegal activities (Ostman, "Total Surveillance," 140).

The bottom line is that an intelligent camera can be programmed to recognize a person's face the minute he walks into a room or zoom in on people who look nervous, angry, or upset. I once walked into a high security room where a camera monitored my every move and videotaped my actions. It was a long narrow room with a video camera obnoxiously placed in the center of a wall aimed at me. All you could hear was the hum of computers in the room, and you had the sense that you were being watched.

After experiencing this and walking around the complex where cameras were being aimed at employees everywhere, I got into a conversation with one of the people in charge. I talked about the fact that a society that believed in absolutes like God and concepts like right and wrong didn't need surveillance cameras aimed at everybody because people could be trusted. I also mentioned how sad it is that in our day, which has rejected these moral laws, nobody can trust anybody anymore, and cameras must be used to control people. In other words, modern man, in a vain attempt to become free, has ended up becoming a slave in a world where technology is increasingly being used to control and monitor human behavior. The person I was talking to seemed excited by the new technology and said, "I believe that these systems free you" because they allow you to trust people. I couldn't help but think how far down the road we have come if the only time we can trust people is when they are being videotaped on camera.

Eye Spy

The Central Intelligence Agency has recently released millions of top secret satellite photos taken from 1960 to 1972. These photos can be used to monitor the effects of environmental pollution on the earth's deserts and tropical rainforests. By today's standards, these Keyhole satellites are somewhat primitive because they could only reveal objects up to 460 feet in size. Today's satellites can reveal objects that are around three inches in size from outer space. Soon the technology will be so sophisticated that they will be able to photograph someone in their backyard having a barbecue and they will be able to tell if your steak is well done or medium rare from a satellite orbiting the earth.

Advanced Keyhole satellites are three-story tall automated telescopes in a low earth orbit that use television cameras that broadcast images instantly to CIA "spy shops" across the globe. This way it is possible to keep track of what is going on in Iran, Russia, or even South Central Los Angeles through satellite technology. It is possible to photograph a street corner drug deal by satellite and watch it going down from some remote location in another corner of the planet (Ralph Vartabedian "Spy Satellite Photos Rich in Data Likely To Be Released," *Los Angeles Times* [14 January 1995]: 18).

A National ID Card

In California during a recent state election, the big

issue was Proposition 187, which led to Gov. Pete Wilson's reelection. Proposition 187 involved denying certain government services to illegal aliens. The whole issue of people illegally coming into the United States has created such a controversy that Texas Congresswoman Barbara Jordan, who heads the U.S. Commission on Immigration Reform, has proposed the idea of a national ID card.

This national ID card would be a computer card that would contain certain key information and be required by employers before hiring anybody for a job. The Defense Department is issuing its new Multi-Technology Automated Reader Card (MARC) to U.S. military personnel through a special program developed by the Pentagon. These MARC cards contain an integrated computer circuit chip and bar code. Military personnel will use it for access to meals and medical care. Likewise, a national ID card would be similar to the military's MARC card (Peter Cassidy, "We Have Your Number," *The Progressive* [December 1994]: 28–29).

When Pres. Bill Clinton proposed his national health care program, Hillary Clinton announced that every U.S. citizen would be given a national health card. In addition, the United States Postal Service announced that it will accept credit cards and possibly its own U.S. Postal Service Card. Furthermore, companies like AT&T are working to expand the use of Smart Cards. Within five years, AT&T believes that consumers will use Smart Cards to purchase stocks, fill out insurance forms, preserve IRS data, tell you how much you have in your savings account, and unlock your front door.

Biometrics

Biometrics is the new technology that gathers biological information such as your DNA code, fingerprints, palm recognition, voice patterns, etc., and records them into computer systems that can identify you. In this "brave new world" technology, your fingerprints, eye movements (or retinal scans), voice, and DNA code can all be used to identify you by computer. Information companies such as TRW provide biometric service bureaus that provide instant access to personal dossier information to business, government, banks, military bases, research facilities, and drug companies.

A major banking group in England has developed a technology called Biocode or Biopin, which is a digitized memory recording that can be used in a Smart Card that can record key information and identify the holder. Through the use of biometric and computer technology, it is now possible to place a miniature microchip in the skin that can keep track of a person's location. Currently this technology is being used to prevent cattle thefts, and it is now being talked about being used in young children to prevent child kidnapping.

The Coming Persecution

In Luke 21:12–19, Jesus Christ clearly warns His followers that in the last days there will be persecution of believers. Even here in America, persecution of believers in Jesus Christ is happening before our very eyes. As society get worse and worse and more involved with evil and immorality, it is going to begin to increasingly hate the people of the Light, who are Christians. The reason for this is that Light that is in us exposes the darkness that is them, and they don't like it.

Our society has become a cesspool of immorality, violence, and perversion. While flipping through the television stations the other day in midafternoon, I heard the detailed testimony of wife-beating, blood, and violence in the O.J. Simpson trial. On another channel, I heard in graphic detail the sexual exploits of Madonna and Elvis Presley. All of these programs aired during the day when young children could be watching them, and they are an open sewer of filth and degradation. Parents allow their children to wear masks with O.J. Simpson and Nicole Simpson as Halloween costumes when they trick or treat.

The lead singer of the rock 'n' roll group Guns 'N' Roses wears a T-shirt with a picture of Charles Manson on it and even recorded a song of Manson's on one of his multi-million-dollar selling albums.

Our own U.S. government through the Equal Employment Opportunity Commission (EEOC) almost passed into law a whole series of regulations in the workplace that would have made it illegal to be openly a Christian. The EEOC would have made it unlawful to wear a cross around the neck; to wear a yarmulke (a Jewish head covering); to have a picture of Jesus Christ on your desk; to have any religious emblem on, such as a fish sign or cross, to display a Bible in the open; to celebrate Christmas, Hannukkah, Thanksgiving, or Easter celebrations; to pray at banquets or events; to share your faith in Christ in any way; or to host a Bible study or prayer breakfast.

This government agency almost succeeded in making it illegal to be a Christian in the workplace. But, this dangerous anti-Christian trend continues to be at work in our society. Two other bills were also passed by Congress that would have severely restricted the freedom of speech of Christians. The first was the so-called Crush Rush bill, which would have forced conservative and Christian radio talk show hosts to give equal time to opposing viewpoints anytime they spoke out against abortion, homosexual rights, or any other social or political issue. This would have literally closed down Christian radio stations across the country. The second bill, which was named Crush Rush II would have forced programs like "Focus on the Family," "Rush Limbaugh," and the "700 Club" to register every single person who watched their programs as political lobbyists with the U.S. government.

These bills would have taken all religious and conservative programs off the air, and the scary thing is that both of these bills could have been passed. After the Oklahoma City bombing, there were many voices blaming Talk Radio for the violence. Again, there was a cry to censor, under the pretense of stopping terrorism, all Talk Radio programs that criticize the government and some of its policies.

Our world is fascinated by evil, and as it moves more into immorality, the occult, and spiritual darkness, it is going to persecute Christians more intensely. If you look at what is happening in America in terms of persecution and hatred of Christians, it is always initiated by people who are involved in immorality, or spiritual darkness.

Jesus Christ told us,

> But before all these things, they will lay hands on you and persecute you, delivering you up to synagogues and prisons. You will be brought before kings and rulers for My names sake. But it will turn out for you as an occasion for testimony. Therefore settle it in your hearts not to meditate before hand on what you will answer; for I will give you a mouth and wisdom which all your adversaries will not be able to contradict and resist. You will be betrayed even by parents and brothers, relatives and friends; and they will put some of you to death. (Luke 21:12–16)

Chapter Sixteen

Prophetic Fulfillment in Israel

Israel is God's prophetic time clock. Although the original Israel was dissolved centuries ago, in 1948 the new nation of Israel was reestablished. The regathering of the Jews to Israel is a clear prophetic sign in the Old and New Testament of the soon return of the Messiah, Jesus Christ. On 6 June 1967, the Jews recaptured Jerusalem in the Six-Day War. It was the first time that the Jews had control over Jerusalem since before Nebuchadnezzar captured the city in 586 B.C. Many Bible scholars believe that the Six-Day War in 1967 marks the end of what is called the Gentile world power.

Romans 11:25 states, "For I do not desire, brethren, that you should be ignorant of this mystery, lest you should be wise in your own opinion, that blindness in part has happened to Israel until the fullness of the Gentiles has come in." The Bible teaches us that Israel's rejection of Jesus as the Messiah is only temporary, and the time will come when many in Israel will accept Jesus as Lord.

Dr. Jack W. Hayford gave a special sermon on 15 January 1995 entitled "Exciting Things—What's Happening In Israel," in which he detailed some of the remarkable things that are happening in the nation of Israel in the fulfillment of Zechariah 12:1–12, Zechariah 13:1–2, and Romans 11. According to Dr. Hayford, there are now over twenty Messianic congregations in Israel that are pastored by Israeli Jews who believe that Jesus is the Messiah. In addition, there are now about four to five thousand believers in Israel who are Israeli citizens, and almost everyday a Jewish Israeli is receiving Jesus as Messiah.

These are remarkable developments because during the past twenty-five years most Israeli Jews were indifferent or hostile towards the gospel of Jesus Christ. However, during the last two or three years, there has been a spiritual openness from the Jews that is nothing short of miraculous. In fact, there is a transformation going on in Israel that is truly amazing. The very fact that Israel is open to peace talks represents a fundamental change in their attitude and the spiritual climate.

In Romans 11:11–15, the Apostle Paul writes,

> I say then, they have stumbled that they should fall? Certainly not! But through their fall, to provoke them to jealousy, salvation has come to the Gentiles. Now if their fall is riches for the world, and their failure riches for the Gentiles, how much more their fullness. For I speak to you Gentiles; inasmuch as I am an apostle to the Gentiles, I magnify my ministry, if by any means I may provoke to jealousy those who are my flesh and save some of them. For if their being cast away is the reconciling of the world, what will their acceptance be but life from the dead.

The rejection of Jesus as Messiah by the Jews has caused the Gentile world to be able to receive Jesus Christ as their Savior. According to Paul, God's plan is that, when the unbelieving Jews see the Gentiles turn to Christ, they will become spiritually jealous and turn to Christ also. The Apostle Paul talks about a time of a future revival among the Jews, which he terms "their fullness." Paul speaks of a future time when the spiritual "blindness" of the Jews will end; this time will be when the "fullness of the Gentiles has come in."

In the above verses, Paul is speaking of a time when there will be a massive gathering of Jews who come to accept Jesus Christ as their Messiah. In Zechariah 12:2–

5, the prophet Zechariah, who began his ministry in 520
B.C., wrote:

> "Behold, I will make Jerusalem a cup of drunken-
> ness to all the surrounding peoples, when they lay
> siege against Judah and Jerusalem. And it shall
> happen in that day that I will make Jerusalem a
> very heavy stone for all peoples; all who would
> heave it away will surely be cut in pieces, though all
> the nations of the earth are gathered against it. In
> that day," says the Lord, "I will strike every horse
> with confusion, and its rider with madness; I will
> open My eyes on the house of Judah, and will
> strike every horse of the people with blindness.
> And the governors of Judah shall say in their heart,
> 'The inhabitants of Jerusalem are my strength and
> the Lord of hosts, their God.' "

There is coming a time when all the nations will be
gathered against Jerusalem. Ezekiel 38 outlines a scenario when the nations of the earth will be gathered against
Israel. It is not hard to imagine some organization like
the United Nations or a Russian-led force mobilizing a
strike against Israel. Yet, this will also be a time of spiritual revival for God's people.

Zechariah 12:10 states, "And I will pour on the house
of David and on the inhabitants of Jerusalem the Spirit of
grace and supplication; then they will look on Me whom
they pierced. Yes, they will mourn for Him as one mourns
for His only son, and grieve for Him as one grieves for
a firstborn." Five hundred years before the coming of
Jesus Christ, Zechariah prophesies about a time when
Israel will have their eyes opened and accept the Messiah
that they have rejected.

This spiritual revival among the Jews is supposed to
occur in the time period when all the nations will attack
Israel in some kind of future battle. Could it be that we
are rapidly approaching the time when Israel will be invaded by an alliance of nations? Are we nearing the fulfillment of Ezekiel 38?

Zechariah continues by saying, "'In that day a fountain shall be opened for the house of David and for the inhabitants of Jerusalem, for sin and uncleanness. It shall be in that day,' says the Lord of hosts, 'that I will cut off the names of idols from the land, and they shall no longer be remembered. I will cause the prophets and the unclean spirit to depart from the land'" (Zech. 13:1–2). When the Jews accept Jesus as their Messiah, a cleansing fountain of spiritual revival will break forth.

In Romans 11, the Apostle Paul reminds us that when the Jews rejected Jesus, it resulted in a great spiritual blessing to the rest of the world who then had an opportunity to receive Jesus Christ as their Savior. However, when the Jews accept Jesus as their Messiah, which Paul refers to as "their fullness," there will be a great move of God's Spirit throughout the world. Dr. Jack Hayford believes that when Israel opens to Jesus Christ there will be a new sweep of God's Spirit that will surge out into the world. A new dimension of the gospel will be released, and it will cause an explosion of the gospel to all mankind.

The Miracle of Israel

Ezekiel 38:8 gives a prophecy about a future time when Jews will once again return to their homeland. "After many days you will be visited. In the latter years you will come back into the land of those brought back from the sword and gathered from many people on the mountains of Israel, which had long been desolate; they were brought out of the nations, and now all of them dwell safely." After nearly two thousand years, Israel has once again become a nation where millions of Jews around the world are coming to live.

In 1939 the largest single Jewish community was in the United States and over 9.5 million Jews were living in Europe in nations such as Poland, the USSR, Romania, Hungary, Czechoslovakia, Austria, etc. Adolf Hitler reduced the world's Jewish population by over 6 million people between 1939 and 1945. And, ever since that time,

Europe ceased being the center of Jewish life. Today, the vast majority of Jews live either in Israel or the United States (Robert Wistrich, "Do The Jews Have A Future?" *Commentary* [July 1994]).

There are an estimated four hundred thousand to over one million Jews living in the former Soviet Union. Many of those people are strongly considering relocating to Israel as tensions mount in Russia. Antisemitism is once again raising its ugly head. The prophet Jeremiah may have had this Russian exodus in mind when he said,

> "Therefore, behold, the days are coming," says the Lord, "that they shall no longer say, 'As the Lord lives who brought up the children of Israel from the land of Egypt,' but, 'As the Lord lives who brought up and led the descendants of the house of Israel from the north country and from all the countries where I had driven them.' And they shall dwell in their own land." (Jer. 23:7–8)

The Six-Day War in 1967 was a turning point for the nation of Israel when they recaptured Jerusalem. Outnumbered and outgunned, it was nothing short of a miracle that the Jews were able to so swiftly regain control of it. It was the first time the Jews had lasting control of the city since the Babylonian destruction in the sixth century B.C.

Shake, Rattle, and Roll

In Ezekiel 37, the prophet Ezekiel, whose name means "God strengthens," gives a prophecy of a time when dry bones will come to life again. Ezekiel, who was called by God in 593 B.C., gives a prophecy of a future time when the nation of Israel will come alive again spiritually and believe in Jesus as the Messiah. It is interesting to note that this prophecy of Ezekiel 37 occurs right before the prophecy of the War of Gog and Magog in Ezekiel 38.

Bible teacher and prophecy expert David Hocking gave a special New Year's Eve message in 1994 with the founder of Calvary Chapel, Chuck Smith, on Israel, prophecy, and one-world government. Both Smith and Hocking affirmed the role of Israel in biblical prophecy and pointed to the fact that the restoration of Israel in 1948, the Six-Day War in 1967, and the current plans to rebuild the temple are all part of an end-times prophetic scenario. These men stressed the fact that Israel plays a key role in Bible prophecy and that recent events in the Middle East point to the fulfillment of biblical prophecy. In 1948 David Ben Gurion decided to call Palestine *Israel* as a fulfillment of Ezekiel 37:12 which states, " 'Therefore prophesy and say to them,' thus says the Lord God: 'Behold, O My people, I will open your graves and cause you to come up from your graves and bring you to the land of Israel.' "

Recently, more than three thousand people who were Auschwitz survivors gathered at the fiftieth anniversary of their liberation in Jerusalem. An estimated 1.5 million people died at Auschwitz. The pain of this reunion was amplified by the fact that two terrorist suicide bombers had blown themselves up near the coastal town of Netanya, killing nineteen people and wounding sixty more. Of the Holocaust survivors, over 5,550,000 made their way to Palestine, which became Israel in 1948. In the early 1950s Holocaust survivors made up one-third of the Jewish population. Today, about three hundred thousand Holocaust survivors are still alive in Israel and they represent about 45 percent of the nation's elderly population (Mary Curtis, "Auschwitz Is Remembered by Israeli Survivors," *Los Angeles Times*, 23 January 1995).

It is nothing short of miraculous that the Jewish Holocaust survivors would end up living in the prophetic rebirth of the Israel of 1948. It is no accident that after madman Adolf Hitler's Nazi Germany was crushed by the Allied Forces that Israel was reborn shortly after. Israel is God's prophetic time clock, and we are living in a time when it appears that we could possibly see the fulfillment of Ezekiel 38.

The rebirth of Israel is nothing short of a miracle. In fact, there are many aspects of Israel's existence that are miraculous. Ezekiel 36:8 states, "But you, O mountains of

Israel, you shall shoot forth your branches and yield your fruit to My people Israel, for they are about to come." Today, Israel has become the third largest grower of fruit after the United States and Canada. About 80 percent of the European Common Market's fruit comes from Israel.

Yet, only a short time ago Israel was a desert that was practically barren. The Jews have planted billions of trees over the last several decades, and Israel has become a fruitful and productive nation as prophesied by Ezekiel 36:8. Amos 9:13–15 states,

> "Behold, the days are coming," says the Lord, "When the plowman shall overtake the reaper, and the treader of grapes him who sows seed; the mountains shall drip sweet wine, and all the hills shall flow with it. I will bring back the captives of My people Israel; They shall build the waste cities and inhabit them; they shall also make gardens and eat from them. I will plant them in their land, And no longer shall they be pulled up from the land I have given them," says the Lord your God.

Israel Prepares for Nuclear War

Even as Israel negotiates peace treaties with Syria, Lebanon, Jordan, and the Palestinian Liberation Organization, key leaders are alarmed over the spread of nuclear weapons. Nations like Iraq and Iran have the capability to fire nuclear weapons into the major cities of Israel. Prime Minister Yitzhak Rabin was deeply concerned about the rising tide of militant Islamic fundamentalism and he believes that Iran is one of the primary nations responsible for spreading militant Islamic fundamentalism. The goal of militant Islamic fundamentalism is to destroy the Jewish state and set up a pan-Islamic nation in the region.

Nations like Libya, Iran, and Syria have acquired nuclear technology as well as chemical warfare. In addition, these nations are developing intermediate-range nuclear weapons that could strike Israel from a distance. In response, Israel has initiated a five-year plan to beef up its strategic forces by buying the most advanced weapons it can get from the United States and other sources. Israel is increasing its armored units and buying attack helicopters, multiple rocket launchers, and computer-guided bombs and rockets.

Some Israeli generals have called for the development of airborne commando units that can fly into Iran and Iraq at a moment's notice and strike deep into the heart of these nations. Even if Israel succeeds in making peace with some of its neighbors, they would still be susceptible to missile attacks along with biological, chemical, and nuclear weapons from countries like Iran and Iraq.

Military experts such as U.S. Defense Secretary William Perry do not believe that Iran has yet developed an atomic bomb. Perry thinks that Iran is fifteen years away from making an effective A-bomb. But, other experts believe that Iran may be able to acquire an atomic bomb in the near future. In 1981, a bombing of Iraq's Osirak nuclear plant slowed down their nuclear development, but the Chinese and Russians are currently building nuclear reactors in Iran with a three hundred-megawatt nuclear reactor to be built by the Chinese in just six years.

Israel is believed to have over two hundred nuclear warheads and refuses to sign the Nuclear Non-Proliferation Treaty and is preparing to dominate "the future battlefield." In 1996 the Israeli airforce will have F-151 planes, which can fly into Iran, Iraq, Syria, and Algeria in the dark without the need to refuel and can carry over eleven tons of bombs and missiles. In addition, Israel is developing the Arrow antimissile system to intercept and destroy incoming ballistic missiles. During the Gulf War, Israel was hit by thirty-nine missiles, and they do not want to ever be vulnerable to that kind of attack again. Israel is also getting its hands on Apache helicopters, Dolphin-class submarines from Germany, and highly advanced early warning radar systems (Michael Parks, "Israel Looks Past Borders, Arms for Long-Range War," *Los Angeles Times*, 5 February 1995).

Chapter Seventeen

The Role of Islam

The goal of Iran's leader Hashamir Rafsanjani is to get the Western nations out of the Middle East and take control over Jerusalem. Iran is attempting to use Islamic fundamentalism as the means to mobilize a force against Israel. The goal of Islamic leaders such as Rafsanjani is to unite all Islamic nations into a crescent that extends from Indonesia in the Pacific Ocean to Tunisia in the Atlantic Ocean. Islamic fundamentalism is a powerful organizing force which may well be one of the key factors that enables Russia along with a host of Islamic nations to conduct a massive military operation against Israel as described in Ezekiel 38.

The religion of Islam was founded by the prophet Muhammad, born on 22 April A.D. 570 to Amina bint Wahb and her husband Abdullah, who were part of a merchant tribe of Quraish in Mecca which was a trading post in Arabia. Mecca was also the center of idol worship at the sanctuary of Kaaba, which was a small square temple containing a sacred black stone, which historians believe was a fallen meteorite.

In A.D. 613, Muhammad began to receive so-called divine revelations and began to preach his message of Allah. He then began to organize an army of Islamic followers who would shout "Allahu Akbar!" which means "God is Great!"—the battle cry of Islam. Around A.D. 634 to A.D. 638 Syria, Persia, and Iraq began to fall under Muslim attack. And, in A.D. 638 Jerusalem was conquered by Muslim forces.

Today, Islam has over one billion followers, and it is growing rapidly. It has spread throughout Africa into Morocco, Algeria, Libya, Egypt, Chad, Sudan, and down as far as South Africa. It is a major force in every nation of Africa. It is also the most powerful force in the Middle East in nations such as Turkey, Syria, Iraq, Saudi Arabia, Kuwait, Iran, and Jordan. Its influence has spread into Pakistan, Sri Lanka, Bangaladesh, Malayasia, and Indonesia. Islam is also a key factor in the southern part of what used to be the USSR. Since the dismantling of the Russian Empire, Islamic fundamentalism appears to have replaced Marxism as the number one ideological force (Dilip Hiro, *Holy Wars: The Rise of Islamic Fundamentalism*, [Routledge, New York: Routledge, 1989] and Jacques Jomier, *How To Understand Islam* [New York: Crossroad 1991]).

The third holiest city of Islam is Jerusalem and they would like to have it under their control. The loss of Jerusalem to the Christians in the First Crusade in 1095 to A.D. 1099 created a crisis in the Islamic world. Although the Muslims maintain the Dome of the Rock in Jerusalem, they would like to have all of Israel and Jerusalem under their dominion.

To Islamic fundamentalists, the United States is the Great Satan, and they are engaged in an Islamic war against the United States and Israel. In 1974 Yassar Arafat issued a charter that called for the extermination of Israel off the face of the earth. To date, he has not yet repudiated that statement. Islamic nations like Iran, Iraq, Libya, Sudan, and Syria are committed to terrorism. In fact, it has been alleged that Assad of Syria supports a large number of Middle Eastern terrorist groups. In addition, authorities suspect that Assad is responsible for 80 percent of the drug problem in Europe by smuggling drugs like cocaine in huge quantities. Ironically, the U.S. State Department as well as Europe continues to negotiate with these people.

Recently, the U.S. Congress gave over $500 million to the Palestinian Liberation Organization, which Israel believes was used to support terrorist groups. Yet, our own FBI and CIA, which has agreed to no longer spy on Russia, has now officially decided to set up intelligence activities in Israel in order to spy on Israel. It seems that as global pressures increase and the new world order is put in place that Israel is becoming, as the prophet declared, a "cup of stumbling for the nations."

Islamic fundamentalism is the key ingredient in mobilizing military aggression against Israel and the United States. Iran's Hashamir Rafsanjani is attempting to organize an Islamic crescent in order to eliminate the West from the Middle East and take over Jerusalem.

Islamic Terrorism

It appears we are on the very edge of the kind of scenario outlined in Ezekiel 38 and 39, in which Israel is invaded by Russia in the north and an alliance of Middle Eastern nations. In recent years there has been a new wave of Islamic terrorism launched against the nation of Israel. In Afulah on 6 April 1994 a bomb next to a bus killed eight people; in Haderah a few weeks later a bomb on a bus killed five people; in Beit Lid on 22 January 1995 two bombs placed at a junction slaughtered twenty-one people; in Tel Aviv a bomb on a bus killed twenty-two; in Jerusalem there was an attempted bus bombing; and, in Netzarim a bicycle bomber killed three people.

With the continued rise of militant Islamic fundamentalism in some quarters, the danger of terrorist attacks grows daily. Intelligence reports indicate that young children in some Islamic nations are being trained as suicide bombers who will physically carry bombs into Israel and kill themselves in the service of Allah.

The leader of the Islamic Jihad, Dr. Fathi Shikaki, who boasted publicly that the Islamic Jihad was responsible for the suicide attack on Beit Lid, has said, "Peace will not last in this area as long as there is an Israeli State"

(Linda Scherzer, "Boastful Confidence in Damascus," *Jerusalem Report* [23 February 1995]: 16). According to the *Jerusalem Report*, Dr. Fathi Shikaki is dedicated to destroying the Jewish state and says, "No matter if it takes one generation or three, our sons and grandsons will complete what we have started" (ibid.). Shikaki reveals the mindset of some Islamic fundamentalists who are bent on destroying Israel at any cost. There can be no lasting peace in the Middle East as long as this belief system remains ingrained in the minds of some militants.

The Bible teaches that in the last days, this hostility towards Israel is going to increase to such a point that it literally triggers Armageddon. Zechariah 12:2 states, "Behold, I will make Jerusalem a cup of drunkenness to all the surrounding peoples, when they lay siege against Judah and Jerusalem."

In an effort to stop terrorists from coming from the West Bank into Israel, Prime Minister Yitzhak Rabin has even talked of building a gigantic fence costing hundreds of millions of dollars. Shimon Romah, a former senior Shin Bet operative said, "If the fence means that even one suicide bomber can't get through, then many lives can be saved, and its worthwhile" (ibid., 13).

Prime Minister Rabin initiated a "four pronged approach" to dealing with Islamic Jihad and Hamas bombers. It consists of demanding increased cooperation from Yasser Arafat's Palestinian Authority, building the massive security fence on the West Bank, upping intelligence gathering reports inside Gaza and the West Bank, and going after known Hamas and Islamic Jihad-linked groups in the West Bank.

However, Islamic extremists may be able to get a hold of highly destructive Stinger, shoulder-held anti-aircraft missiles that the CIA gave to the Mujahedin. In addition, there are an estimated fifteen thousand nuclear mines and artillery shells in the republics of the former Soviet Union. Some of these republics are Muslim, where Islamic terrorists may find ready sellers who sympathize in their cause. If nuclear mines and artillery shells go off, they could trigger an Israeli retaliation, which could escalate into World War III.

Black Gold

Many of the militant Islamic nations seem to have an endless supply of wealth that comes from oil money. One time while on business, I had the opportunity to visit one of the many homes of a Middle Eastern prince who was worth billions of dollars. This prince had an estate the size of a hotel in Bel Air, California, just down the street from Ronald and Nancy Reagan and across the way from Elizabeth Taylor. As I drove into the large complex, security cameras followed my every move. When I emerged from the car, there were dozens of Americans who looked like clean-cut FBI agents everywhere with earphones in their ears and guns strapped to their sides.

This wealthy Arab prince flew into the United States in his own private jumbo jet, accompanied by his required private army. He would live in this estate for only a few months to entertain his many friends, and he had similar mansions all across the world. There are very few Americans who could have afforded that home. Only billionaires rich from oil money can amass the enormous wealth to hire private armies to protect them and their large estates.

Many of the Organization of Petroleum Exporting Countries (OPEC) are militantly Islamic. Tragically, funds produced from these oil-rich nations are sometimes used to finance operations that are anti-Israeli and terrorist in nature.

Iraq

If you thought the Gulf War and Operation Desert Storm defeated Saddam Hussein, you were wrong. President Clinton dispatched the four thousand member "ready brigade" of the Twenty-fourth Mechanized Infantry Division along with its special M-1A2 tanks to keep Saddam in his place. In addition, two hundred Tomahawk missiles would be aimed at Baghdad in an effort to contain Saddam.

Although President Bush launched an impressive military operation against Saddam Hussein, over half of his armed forces are intact. Prior to Desert Storm, Hussein had 1,200,000 troops. However, he still has almost half a million troops left. In addition, Saddam still has over 2,100 tanks; 2,700 personnel carriers; 1,900 artillery pieces; 2 warships; 6 bombers; 130 strike aircraft; 180 jet fighters; 120 attack helicopters; 22 Scud launchers and 600 SAMs, according to the U.S. Defense Department. This is a pretty sizable military for a guy who was supposedly defeated (John Barry and Russell Watson, "On alert for Desert Storm II," *Newsweek* [17 October 1994]: 29–30).

The ancient city of Babylon was located in modern Iraq. Babylon was an ancient-world military, financial, and cultural power that was established by Nimrod, who built the Tower of Babel, and some Bible scholars believe that the Books of Jeremiah, Isaiah, and Revelation predict that ancient Babylon will be rebuilt. Interestingly, Saddam Hussein has spent over $800 million rebuilding Babylon along with the Ishtar Gate, where Daniel and Jewish people passed through.

In Revelation 18:1–24, Babylon represents the world system under the control of Satan. Precisely what role the actual city of Babylon will play is unclear. However, we know that one of the nations spoken about in Ezekiel 38:1–6 is Persia, which is modern Iran, Iraq, and Afghanistan. It could be that the fanatical zeal of Saddam Hussein along with the military might of Iraq will play a key role in this invasion of Israel.

In any case, Iraq has become a key player in any likely end-times scenario. The majority of key law enforcement officers in New York City believe that it was Iraq that was involved in the World Trade Center bombing. And, there is evidence to suggest that Iraq was involved with Sheik Omar and the people who built the twelve hundred pound bomb which was designed to cause one of the World Trade Center towers to crash into the other one killing tens of thousands.

But, the madness doesn't stop there; there is supposedly an Iraqi agent that the intelligence community calls a "sleeper" who is working in the field of genetic engineering somewhere in New York City. Under orders from Iraq, this "sleeper" could be awakened and unleash a biological warfare operation in Manhattan very easily that could infect hundreds of thousands with bacteria cultures like yersinia pestis, bacillus anthracis, vibrio cholera 01, salmonella typhi, or clostridium botulinum.

Despite U.N. Resolution 687, which called for the destruction of Iraq's nuclear infrastructure, it appears that Iraq is still actively developing nuclear weapons. According to *Arms Control Today* (Jon B. Wolfsthal, *Arms Control Today*, Jan./Feb. 1992), Iraq had received help in the past from companies like the U.S. firm Dupont, eight German companies, and a Swiss firm, along with Swedish and Japanese companies who supplied Iraq with components to be used in nuclear technology. Although many of these manufacturers may not have supplied equipment directly to Iraq and may not have known of their intended use, Iraq was still able to secure the parts needed for nuclear weapons.

Through trickery, Iraq was able to build nuclear weapons using natural uranium and parts and technology supplied from the United States Department of Defense, the Atomic Energy Commission of Brazil, the German Arthur Pfeiffer Company, and Swiss companies. Since the United States and other countries needed Iraq because of the threat of Iran, the U.S. government approved the sale of over $1.5 billion in computers, electronic equipment, and machine tools that could be used in a nuclear, chemical, and ballistic missile program. France sold Iraq over $5 billion worth of aircraft and missiles. Then, during the Gulf War, Saddam Hussein turned around and used this technology to fight against the United States and invade Kuwait (David Albright and Mark Hibbs, "Western Nations Contributed to Iraq's Weapons Program" *Nuclear Proliferation* [San Diego: Greenhaven Press, 1992], 120–123).

The U.N. Limits Oil Sales from Iraq

The United Nations has allowed Iraqi President Saddam Hussein over $1 billion in oil every ninety days for the humanitarian needs of its people. Just prior to the Gulf War, Iraq produced 2.8 million barrels of oil a day, and the current U.N. resolution allows Iraq to produce 635,000 barrels per day. Of the $1 billion of oil produced, the United Nations would set aside $300 million for Gulf War reparations and around $50 million for the United Nations.

U.N. Secretary General Boutros Boutros-Ghali described this as a "first step in lifting sanctions against Iraq." France and Russia have been lobbying for an end to all U.N. restrictions on Iraq's exports. However, the U.N. Special Commission on Iraq must feel secure that Iraq has stopped producing nuclear, biological, and chemical weapons of mass destruction (Stanley Meisler, "U.N. Allows Limited Sales of Iraqi Oil," *Los Angeles Times*, 15 April 1995).

Iraq is a nation that will play a key role in Bible prophecy. The ancient city of Babylon, which is located in modern-day Iraq, is currently being rebuilt in Iraq along with its temple. As a political empire, Babylon ended in 539 B.C. when it was overrun by the Medes and Persians and then taken over by Greece and finally Rome. However, Babylon as a city and a religion continued on.

John F. Walvoord author of *Major Bible Prophecies* writes, "The Old Testament abounds with prophecies about Babylon that have not been fulfilled. These include its ultimate destruction as a religion and as a city. While the final world empire is a Roman Empire, in many respects it continues the evil character of the Babylonian

Empire" (John F. Walvoord, *Major Bible Prophecies—37 Crucial Prophecies That Affect You Today* [New York: HarperCollins Publishers, Zondervan Publishing, 1991], 381). It could well be that Babylon's future role in biblical prophecy will largely be financed through its oil exports. According to the Scriptures, Iraq and Babylon have an important role to play in the years ahead.

Chapter Eighteen

The Samson Option

The Israeli army has a code name, the Samson Option, where if things get really tough, they are prepared to take all their enemies down with them in a nuclear holocaust. Like Samson of old who pulled down the pillars of a temple and caused it to crash down and kill his enemies along with himself, the Jewish military will never surrender, but rather will destroy themselves and their enemies.

Leonard Spector, one of the foremost experts on nuclear weapons, believes that Israel has a strong nuclear arsenal and possesses very advanced nuclear weapons (Leonard Spector, *Nuclear Ambitions*, Boulder: Westview Press, 1990). In 1986, a former nuclear scientist Mordechai Vanunu confirmed the existence of Israel's nuclear arsenal. Some of these nuclear devices are of an advanced design that make them many times more powerful than the atomic weapons used in World War II.

Israel has been using enriched uranium and advanced laser technology that has caused them to develop a very sophisticated array of powerful nuclear weapons that, if triggered, could cause a doomsday scenario in the Middle East like the one described in Ezekiel 38. The basic target of Israel's nuclear arsenal is its Arab neighbors. According to Israel's Samson Option Plan, if Israel's enemies launch an attack on Israel, the nation is prepared to launch nuclear artillery shells as a defense. A nuclear exchange of this magnitude would create untold devastation, not only destroying large segments of the Middle East, but also spreading nuclear contamination across the planet.

Israel Betrayed

Israel's former foreign and defense minister, Moshe Arens, charges that former Pres. George Bush and the United States betrayed Israel during the Gulf War. In his book *Broken Covenant—American Foreign Policy and the Crisis between the United States and Israel*, Arens states that in the pursuit of U.S. interests in the Middle East, the Bush administration deliberately refused Israel vital intelligence information and attempted to bring down Israel's democratically elected government.

Arens believes that Yitzhak Rabin and Shimon Peres made concessions to Israel's Arab neighbors that would seriously weaken Israel's military defense. In addition, Arens says that the Bush administration forced Israel into a peace agenda by delaying a $10 billion dollar loan and that when Iraq invaded Kuwait in August of 1990, the United States did not give Israel information regarding Iraqi troop movements and the location of Scud missile movements.

The former defense minister also warns that Yassar Arafat still wants to set up a Palestinian state with Jerusalem as its capital and that Syria's Assad will not settle for less than the total evacuation of Israel from the Golan Heights.

Israel's forty-six-year-long quest for peace started with the 1979 Israeli-Egyptian Treaty, then the 1989 peace initiative, the Madrid Conference in 1991, and the latest peace agreements by Rabin. Arens comments that all of these agreements are now based on the perception that Israel cannot be defeated on the battlefield, and, if that perception ever changes, then war will break out. Furthermore, if Israel's enemies believe that they can defeat her militarily, then all peace agreements with Israel become absolutely meaningless!

Many now believe that some of the recent peace agreements, in which Israel has given up territory in regard to her national security, have jeopardized this perception. I believe that if Israel's enemies think they can conquer Israel on the battlefield, they will attempt an invasion like the one describe in Ezekiel 38. Arens warns that the day is coming when Israel may not be strong enough to defend itself (Moshe Arens, *Broken Covenant—American Foreign Policy and the Crisis between U.S. and Israel* [New York: Simon & Schuster, 1995]).

Chapter Nineteen

Will the Bear Move South?

The USSR has now fragmented into fifteen nations, and the Russia of today is smaller than the Russia that Peter the Great ruled. Currently, Russia has a population of only 60 percent of the United States with an economy that is only a tenth of the size of Western Europe. Yet, Russia is a key player in biblical prophecy and the new world order. It is important to remember that Russia has never dismantled the KGB or its military, which has forty-five thousand nuclear warheads, of which many are still aimed at America!

According to the *Brookings Institute Review* in a study entitled "Reluctant Strategic Alignment" by John Steinbruner (Winter 1995), the United States has spent over $11 trillion in a forty-year period to build up the world's most impressive military machine. Russia, China, Iran, Iraq, Syria, Libya, India, and North Korea combined make up only 20 percent of the U.S. budget. But, even with her own economy in shambles and with the breakup of the USSR, Russia plans to spend $100 billion per year to build up its military machine and maintain an army of 1.5 million troops. The question is, why does Russia need such a massive military machine?

Could it be that Russia, who has been secretly making alliances with Islamic fundamentalist nations, needs this massive army to move southward in an invasion of Israel outlined in Ezekiel 38? The hard-liner Vladimir Volfovich Zhirinovsky in his book *The Last Push to The South*, published in Moscow in 1993, talks about Russian soldiers moving south with tremendous masses of tanks. Despite the failing Russian economy, Russia continues to build up its nuclear arsenal with the production of the SS-25 nuclear missile and the SS-N-20 missile, which can be launched from a submarine.

It is very suspicious that our government continues to send billions of dollars to support Russia and why 250 million Americans remain responsible for the defense of 350 million Europeans and 150 million Russians. Globalists who have influenced American foreign policy have made sure that we are the defenders of Russia, Western Europe and even U.S.-NATO guarantees to Eastern Europe. In addition, we continue to send billions of dollars into Russia and the Third World through the World Bank and the International Monetary Fund.

However, this new world order strategy will not work because, according to Ezekiel 38, Russia and her allies will make a move on Israel in the last days.

The Russian Reactor Deal with Iran

The Russian government has decided to go ahead with the sale of light-water nuclear reactors to Iran despite U.S. protests. Defense Secretary William Perry visited Russia and expressed concerns about the spread of nuclear weapons and the transfer of nuclear technology to Iran. Yet, Russia stands to make between $800 million to $1 billion on the deal with Iran.

There are intelligence reports from Washington that indicate that Tehran has plans to build nuclear bombs. In response, the United States has promised to give the Russian Atomic Energy Commission tens of millions of dollars if they will give up their deal with Iran (Steven Erlanger, *New York Times*, 4 April 1995). Shimon Perez of Israel went on record publicly as stating that "Iran wants to destroy Israel." In addition to Russia, China is also planning to build two nuclear reactors in Iran.

Chechnya and the Eastern Bloc

As the Russian Bear moves into what could possibly be an Ezekiel 38 scenario, a number of startling things are happening. Russia's invasion of Chechnya could well cause a major change in the Russian government and the possible overthrow of Boris Yeltsin. In addition, Chechnya is located towards the south of Russia and is near the Georgia border, which is near Armenia, Azerbaijan, Iran, and Turkey.

The former Eastern Bloc nations still possess a formidable army and are capable of mobilizing this army and moving southward towards Israel. According to the International Institute of Strategic Studies, Russia still has 1.7 million active troops with 2.4 million in reserves; the Ukraine has 517,000 troops with 1 million in reserve; Poland has 283,600 troops with 465,000 in reserve; Romania has 230,500 troops with 427,000 in reserve; Bulgaria has 101,900 troops with 303,000 in reserve; and the Czech Republic, Hungary, Slovakia, Lithuania, Lativia, and Estonia all have standing armies (Dean E. Murphy, "Chechnya Summons Uneasy Memories in former East Bloc," *Los Angeles Times* [14 January 1995]: A2).

Moscow's military move into Chechnya will not threaten relations with NATO and the Atlantic Alliance, which is anxious to maintain good relations with Russia. Clearly, the new world order is not about to chastise Russia as it moves towards some type of global government.

Gog and Magog Attack Israel

In the Book of Ezekiel, written between 593 B.C. and 573 B.C., the prophet Ezekiel was given a prophetic vision from God concerning the restoration of Israel and a great last days invasion of Israel by Gog and his allies. In Ezekiel 38 and 39 we read of the account of the war of Gog and Magog who attack Israel when the nation appears to be dwelling safely.

Ezekiel 38:1–9 gives us an account of this coming invasion:

Now the word of the Lord came to me saying, "Son of man, set your face against Gog, of the land of Magog, the prince of Rosh, Meshech, and Tubal and prophesy against him, and say, 'Thus says the Lord God: Behold, I am against you, O Gog, the prince of Rosh, Meshech and Tubal. I will turn you around, put hooks into your jaws, and lead you out, with all your army, horses and horsemen, all splendidly clothed, a great company with bucklers and shields, all of them handling swords. Persia, Ethiopia, and Libya are with them, all of them with shield and helmet; Gomer and all its troops; the house of Togarmah from the far north and all its troops—many people are with you. Prepare yourself and be ready, you and all your companies that are gathered about you; and be a guard for them. After many days you will be visited. In the latter years you will come into the land of those brought back from the sword and gathered from many people on the mountains of Israel, which had been desolate; they were brought out of the nations, and now all of them dwell safely. You will ascend, coming like a storm, covering the land like a cloud, you and all your troops and many peoples with you.'"

Examining Genesis 10:1–3 we discover that the sons of Noah were Shem, Ham, and Japeth. In addition, the sons of Japeth were Gomer, Magog, Madai, Javan Tubal, Meshech, and Tiras. These sons of Japeth all play a key role in Ezekiel's prophecy concerning the war of Gog and Magog. Examining a map of the nations of Genesis 10, we can see that Magog can be identified as the Scythians, which many Bible scholars believe is modern Russia. In addition, to the east of the house of Togarmah is Persia; Cush to the south is Ethiopia, and Put is Libya. Meshech is the Assyrian "Mushku," and Tubal is the Assyrian "Tabab." Persia is the geographic region just east of the Iranian plateau.

Many Bible scholars believe that these nations have specific modern counterparts. For example, Magog is Russia; Persia is Iran, Iraq, and Afghanistan; Ethiopia is both modern Ethiopia and Sudan; Libya would still be Libya; Ashkenaz is Germany and Austria; Gomer is eastern Europe; and Togarmah is southeastern Europe, along with other nations who make up an end-times alliance.

Both Gomer and Togarmah existed in the region of Turkey. Turkey was recently rejected by the European Economic Community for membership in the EEC. As such, Turkey is becoming more of an Islamic state. In 1993 Iran, Syria, and Turkey began uniting due to fears of Kurdistan in northern Iraq. Mumtaz Soysal is Turkey's foreign minister, who is militantly anti-West and has been compared to Russia's Zhirinovsky.

According to Ezekiel, there will be an invasion of Israel by the forces of Magog (Russia), Iran, and other allies from Central Asia in the last days. Nations like Turkey, along with radical Islamic nations, could all play a part in this invasion. It is no accident that Russia has been making secret deals with Islamic countries in what could be preparation for the scenario in Ezekiel 38.

Who Is Gog?

Ezekiel 38 describes what could be a nuclear assault against the modern nation of Israel led by a leader called Gog of the land of Magog. Ancient historians have identified Magog as the Scythians, which is modern Russia. But, the identity of Gog has remained puzzling for many. *New York Times* best-selling author Hal Lindsey and international business executive and prophecy expert Chuck Missler have put forth an interesting theory on the identity of Gog. By going to the Septuagint translation of the Old Testament, Amos 7:1 states, "Thus the Lord showed me, and behold a swarm of locusts were coming, and behold, one of the young devastating locusts was Gog, the king."

Revelation 9:11 also describes a king of the locusts who is "the angel of the bottomless pit, whose name in Hebrew is Abaddon, but in Greek he has the name Apollyon." The passage in Amos 7:1 shows us that this being named Gog is king of the locusts. These locusts are actually demons, and Revelation 9:11 gives us a deeper understanding of this being Gog by calling him Abaddon, which means "Destruction," and Apollyon, which means "Destroyer." Proverbs 30:27 tells us that the locusts are not physical locusts but demonic forces under the leadership of an angel named Abaddon or Gog! Proverbs 30:27 states, "The locusts have no king," and it appears to indicate that these are not natural locusts but demons.

The Bible clearly teaches us that there is an invisible realm, or spiritual world, in which is the unseen. If we read Daniel 10 we find out about powerful spiritual beings such as the Prince of Persia and the Prince of Greece. These are not earthly leaders but evil angels who have been given authority by Satan over certain territories on earth.

Some people have labeled these beings "territorial spirits" and the Bible seems to indicate that above earthly rulers are angelic beings who can exercise control over geographic regions and nations. Principalities and powers can control and dominate nations and national issues. Some of these angelic princes such as the Prince of Persia and the Prince of Greece actually rule over nations.

It is important when discussing such issues that the Bible never calls us to fatalism regarding the reality of principalities and powers in the invisible realm. Paul reminds us in 2 Corinthians 10:3–4 that "though we walk in the flesh, we do not war according to the flesh. For the weapons of our warfare are not carnal but mighty in God for pulling down strongholds." Then, in Ephesians 6:12, Paul says, "For we do not wrestle against flesh and blood, but against principalities, against powers, against the rulers of darkness of this age, against spiritual hosts of wickedness in the heavenly places."

God's people are never to be passive in the face of spiritual forces of evil but to engage in spiritual warfare through prayer, intercession, praise, and worship. Strongholds can be dismantled in the invisible realm and the destiny of individual lives and nations changed as the result of intercessory prayer. God does not reveal to us the reality of principalities and powers to titillate us but rather to enlist us in spiritual warfare.

Chapter Twenty

Future Warfare

As we talk about the War of Gog and Magog and the Armageddon, it is important that we understand just how high-tech modern warfare really is. We all got a glimpse of just how far advanced military technology has progressed during the Gulf War. With amazing accuracy, computers guided missiles into the windows of enemy installations and satellite cameras gave us a bird's eye view of what was happening on the ground.

Modern technology has rocketed our world into cyberspace. Computer technology has revolutionized our society and the way we wage war. Even during the O.J. Simpson trial, which was being televised around the globe, defense team lawyers utilized the very latest in computer technology to pinpoint where O.J. was during the night Nicole Simpson was murdered. Computer generated images gave us aerial views of O.J.'s estate and Nicole's condominium. The same technology is now available to analyze battlefields, and the computer technician is more essential to a military operation than the armed soldier.

In fact, according to a report in *Popular Science* called "Digital Warrior," the most important weapon on today's battlefield is the computer. Futurists Alvin and Heidi Toffler believe that a new arms race is about to dawn on the planet with new weapons that minimize instead of maximize lethal force so that armies can more precisely control the extent of their damage. These weapons include acoustic wave guns, which can stun their adversaries; chemicals that can stop motor vehicles; and computerized camouflage. In the Hollywood movie *Predator*, aliens were able to constantly make themselves invisible through a strange power. Similarly, the U.S. Army hopes to use computer technology to camouflage military movements.

The U.S. Army plans to spend between $5 billion and $10 billion in battlefield computers and virtual reality warfare simulators. Computer-controlled robot tanks will roam enemy territory, and foot soldiers will carry miniature backpack computers with sensors built into their uniforms (Judith Gunther, Suzanne Kantra, and Robert Langreth, "Digital Warrior," *Popular Science* [September 1994]: 60–62).

When we read a passage in Scripture like Revelation 9:1–11, which describes locusts who are like horses prepared for battle with heads wearing crowns that look like gold and the sound of chariots with many horse running into battle with tails like scorpions that can hurt men. This could be a description of demonic warfare or a future kind of warfare with high-tech weapons. Perhaps John caught a glimpse of modern warfare. From his perspective in A.D. 70 to 95, it would have been difficult to describe modern warfare. He would have had to use the kind of picturesque language found in Revelation 9.

Armageddon

Revelation 16:16 states, "And they gathered them together to the place called in Hebrew Armageddon." The War of Armageddon is going to be the final end-times war where demonic spirits, Satan, Anti-christ, and the False Prophet supernaturally organize a great army to attack Israel. Armageddon is located in the northern part of the plains of Jezreel, and *Armageddon* or *Harmageddon* is from the Hebrew root, which means to "arah," which means "to gather, pluck, cut off," and "to slay." In the Old Testament numerous battles were fought here, and the prophet Joel referred to this valley as "the valley of Jehoshaphat" (Joel 3:12).

In Joel 3:9–15, the ancient biblical prophet declares,

Proclaim this among the nations: "Prepare for war! Wake up the mighty men, let all the men of war draw near, let them come up. Beat your plowshares into swords and your pruning hooks into spears; Let the weak say, 'I am strong.' " Assemble and come, all you nations, and gather together all around. Cause your mighty ones to go down there, O Lord. "Let the nations be weakened, and come to the Valley of Jehoshaphat; For there I will sit to judge all the surrounding nations. Put in the sickle, for the harvest is ripe. Come, go down; For the winepress is full, the vats overflow—for their wickedness is great." Multitudes, multitudes in the valley of decision! For the day of the Lord is near in the valley of decision. For the sun and the moon will grow dark, and the stars will diminish their brightness.

There are a couple of things to note in the above passage from Joel. First of all, the new world order is destined to utterly fail. On the cornerstone of the United Nations there is a quote from Isaiah 2:4, which states, "They shall beat their swords into plowshares, and their spears into pruning hooks; nation shall not lift up sword against nation, neither shall they learn war anymore."

The plans of the United Nations and the new world order are going to collapse because the prophet Joel states, "Beat your plowshares into swords and your pruning hooks into spears" (Joel 3:10). There can be no real peace on earth without the Prince of Peace, Jesus Christ, ruling and reigning. Armageddon is going to be the fruit of mankind's disobedience to God.

What Joel was talking about seems to parallel what the Apostle John saw in Revelation 6:12–13, which states, "I looked when He opened the sixth seal, and behold, there was a great earthquake; and the sun became black as sackcloth of hair, and the moon became like blood. And the stars of heaven fell to the earth, as a fig tree drops its late figs when it is shaken by a mighty wind." Both Joel, who saw his vision around 800 B.C., and John, who saw his vision around A.D. 80, may have had a terrifying glimpse of the future when a global thermonuclear war was taking place.

These descriptions of the sun growing dark and the moon becoming blood-red could describe the aftereffects of a global nuclear strike with what scientists call a nuclear winter. Revelation 6:14 states, "Then the sky receded as a scroll when it is rolled up, and every mountain and island was moved out of its place," a description that could possibly fit an atomic blast going off.

The war of Armageddon is going to be the world's great fear of nuclear holocaust being realized. The enormous stockpiles of nuclear weapons that the world has built up for the last several decades could be unleashed all at once at Armageddon. Like some kind of Satanic pinball machine, limited nuclear exchange could easily end up lighting up the whole earth as computer-guided nuclear missiles retaliate against nuclear strikes. The very idea of an all-out nuclear exchange during Armageddon is so horrifying that it is difficult to imagine it without becoming physically ill.

Neo-fascism, the Russian Agenda, and Ezekiel 38

Throughout Europe and Russia, a neo-fascist sentiment is brewing once again. In Germany neo-Nazis organize and publish pamphlets like *Der Enblick* (*Insight*), which is a hit list of German liberals or "enemies who must be eliminated." In Italy neo-fascist leader Gianfranco Fini and the MSI (Italian Socialist movement) are growing in numbers. In Russia, Vladimir Zhirinovsky makes racist remarks and has often been anti-Semitic. In the book *Zhirinovsky-Russian Fascism and the Making of a Dictator*, the authors Vladimir Solovyov and Elena Klepikova write, "Zhirinovsky's anti-Jewish statements vary from announcing the inevitable exodus of Jews from Russia to his proposal for the Jewish question on an international scale: gathering all the Jews on islands . . . He even has specific islands in mind" (Reading, Mass: Addison Wesley [1995], 34).

Many compare Russia to the German Weimar Republic of the 1920s with Zhirinovsky like a new Hitler attempting to take control. The fourteen other republics that once formed the Soviet Union are nervous about someone like Vladimir Zhirinovsky attempting to put the Soviet Empire back again.

Although the "ethnic cleansing" of Moscow began in 1991 and although anti-Semitism has been somewhat cooled by the mass exodus of Jews from the former Soviet Union, both anti-Semitism and other forms of racism brew beneath the surface. With Russia's economy crumbling and the rise of Russian hard-liners like Zhirinovsky, the threat of Russian expansionism and the fulfillment of Ezekiel's prophecy in Ezekiel 38 have become a potential reality.

Russia has signed a military assistance pact with the Central Asian republics of Kazakhstan, Turkmenistan, Tadzikistan, Uzbekistan, and Kirghizia. Could these alliances with the Central Asian republics and Iran fueled by Russian anti-Semitism plus Islamic fundamentalism become the "hooks in the Jaw" written about in Ezekiel 38?

According to business executive-turned-prophecy analyst Chuck Missler, FEMA, or the Federal Emergency Management Agency, has a $1.3 billion program to prepare for a nuclear hit on the United States ("Personal Update," *The Newsletter of Koininia House*, vol. 3, no. 4 [April 1993]). FEMA is the same federal agency that helped to manage the crisis of the Northridge earthquake. According to Missler, it is not earthquakes or floods, but preparations for nuclear war that have accounted for more than 78 percent of FEMA's budget. Missler asks the question, "Is there a tie-in between these preparations and our 12 year covert buildup of Saudi Arabia? Or our operations in the Persian Gulf? Or the present ones in the Red Sea, using Somalia as a cover?"

Anti-Semitism and the
Protocols of the Wise Men of Zion

All over the Islamic countries and the Middle East, there is a rapid increase in the spread of anti-Semitic literature. Surprisingly enough, Japan has now become one of the major centers for the distribution of anti-Semitic materials with an increasing number of bookstores devoted to material that is anti-Jewish and anti-Israel. In the Middle East and Islamic nations, one book that is enjoying a resurgence of popularity is the infamous *The Protocols of the Wise Men of Zion*, which was used by Adolf Hitler and the Third Reich as anti-Semitic propaganda.

The Protocols of the Wise Men of Zion was an appendix work to a book called *The Anti-Christ*, and it was written by an evil Russian writer named Nilus. It was a forged document that was filled with lies, racism, and anti-Semitism. It was supposed to be a record of the proceedings of the World Congress of Jewry held in Basel in 1897 which falsely accused the Jews of laying out a plan for world domination. Although it was evident that the document was a total forgery, it was used by Adolf Hitler as a powerful piece of anti-Semitic propaganda.

Alfred Rosenberg, despite his Jewish ancestry, gained entrance into the secret German occult society led by Dietrich Eckart called the Thulle Gesellschaft, which helped put Hitler into power. The Thulle Gesellschaft then used an independent publisher to distribute the work around Germany. *The Protocols of the Wise Men of Zion* was then distributed around the world, and today it is once again fanning the fuels of anti-Semitism in Europe, Japan, Russia, and the United States, along with Islamic and Middle Eastern nations.

The groundwork for *The Protocols* was originally written as a satire by a French lawyer, Maurice Joly, who wanted to ridicule the political goals of Napoleon III. Joly's work was entitled *Dialogue aus anfers entre Machiaval et Montesquieu, ou la politique de Machiavel au XIX siecle, par un Contemporian*, or *Dialogue in Hell between Machiavelli and Montesquieu, or the politics of Machiavelii in the Nineteenth Century, by a Contemporary.* Joly who was a member of the ancient occult Rosicrucian Order warned of a time when government might use mass communication to control the masses. This material was twisted and distorted by the Ochrana, who were the Tsarist Secret Police in Russia. They used it in an attempt to blame the Marxist Revolution as an international conspiracy by the Jews. This material was eventually recreated as *The Protocols* and brought from Russia to Munich by Alfred Rosenberg in 1918 (Trevor Ravenscroft, *The Spear of Destiny* [Maine: Samuel Weiser, Inc., 1991]).

A writer named Nilus was selected by the Ochrana to write *The Protocols* in an attempt to please the tsar of Russia. However, the tsar recognized it as a forgery, and Nilus was disgraced. Yet, this forged document continues to be the source of enormous anti-Semitic propaganda across the globe even today. In Russia, there is a whole new wave of anti-Semitism, along with Germany, Japan, and the Middle East.

Even here in the United States I have seen some written material and videos by so-called Christian groups that were based on this deceptive information in an attempt to spread anti-Semitism. All of this material is Satanic in nature and flows directly out of Satan's absolute hatred of the Jewish people. It is being used in the Middle East by those who hate Israel in an effort to mobilize the kind of attack on Israel described in Ezekiel 38. Anti-semitism, like any form of racism, is always evil. Real Christians who have the love of Jesus Christ in their hearts must oppose racism in any form. God's love knows no racial or ethnic boundaries.

Chapter Twenty-one

Spiritual Deception

O ne of the characteristics of the last days is the increase of spiritual deception. The Apostle John warns us, "Little children, it is the last hour; and as you have heard that the Anti-christ is coming, even now many anti-christs have come by which we know that this is the last hour" (John 2:18). As this world continues to self-destruct, people become desperate for answers. This is why books like *Embraced by the Light*, which deals with a counterfeit of Christ, and television programs like "The Other Side" have become so popular. In addition, psychic networks are flooding television, and there is an explosive interest in the New Age, horoscopes, and other occult ideas.

The Apostle John stated,

> Beloved, do not believe every spirit, but test the spirits, whether they are of God; because many false prophets have gone out into the world. By this you know the Spirit of God: Every spirit that confesses that Jesus Christ has come in the flesh is of God, and every spirit that does not confess that Jesus Christ has come in the flesh is not of God. And this is the spirit of the Anti-christ, which you heard was coming and is now already in the world. (1 John 4:1–3)

There is a growing relationship between New Age/ Eastern mystical religions and the political establishment. President Clinton has turned to motivational guru Tony

Robbins, author of *Awaken the Giant Within*, whose "Un-limited Power" infomercials saturate late night television. Although Robbins has some good ideas, his teaching basically teaches a person to rely on mental power and not God in order to achieve desired goals. And, Hillary Clinton has reportedly been meeting with Marianne Williamson, who is a teacher of the principles outlined in *A Course in Miracles*, which was channeled to its writers by some kind of "spirit guide."

The Clintons are not the only high-level government officials to have embraced New Age and humanistic teachings. Although Ronald Reagan believed in the Bible as well as biblical prophecy, his wife Nancy Reagan was consulting astrologers like Joan Quigley. In fact, Reagan allowed his wife Nancy to influence him, and they planned their official schedules after consulting their astrologer.

Arianna Huffington, who is the wife of Michael Huffington, who ran for the Senate in California, was involved with guru John-Roger. John-Roger, who was formerly a school teacher, was thrown out of a California school for practicing mind-control experiments on his students. He is the coauthor with Peter McWilliams of best-selling books like *Do It!* and *You Can't Afford the Luxury of a Negative Thought* and has appeared on "Larry King" and other national television shows. But, John-Roger's Movement for Spiritual Awareness (MSIA [pronounced messiah]) is a system of occult teachings.

At the United Nations, one of its departments has been printing and distributing literature about the self-proclaimed messiah, Lord Maitreya. Through its Share International organization, the U.N. is promoting Lord Maitreya, who claims to be the Christ. In fact, Share International is headed by Benjamin Creme, the chief spokesperson for Lord Maitreya. Lord Maitreya is the head of a group called the Spiritual Hiearchy of Ascended Masters, and one of their goals is to create a one-world religion under Lord Maitreya, who is also called the Master.

Spiritual deception has infiltrated every level of our society with powerful organizations like Scientology penetrating the entertainment industry and attracting major stars like Tom Cruise. Dr. Deepak Chopra, who is a bestselling author and frequent guest of national television talk shows and is a one-time disciple of Maharishi Mahesh Yogi. The maharishi (Hindu teacher) is the famous guru who lead the Beatles into practicing TM or Transcendental Meditation.

The maharishi also helped form the Natural Law party in England in order to promote his New Age beliefs in government. Beatle George Harrison played at the gala benefit to fund the Natural Law, which was set up to promote over three hundred candidates in the general British election. In 1993 the maharishi announced from his top security base in a converted monastery in Vladrop, Holland, via satellite, his plans to influence elections in Canada, New Zealand, and other nations with his teachings on meditation.

Maharishi has published a newspaper called *World Government News* and has promoted world peace through meditation (Paul Mason, *The Maharishi* [Rockport, Mass.: Element Inc., 1994]). In a subdivision outside of Austin, Texas, Maharishi's Transcendental Meditation Program has created an entire community called Radiance. The sign outside the upper middle class subdivision reads "Welcome to Radiance. An Ideal Village Practicing the Transcendental Meditation Programs."

The maharishi believes that if he can assemble a core group of meditators in geographical regions around the world, that these people will be able to create world peace. The head of the Radiance community, Robert Shaw, even ran for Congress under the Natural Law party.

The World Church Movement

In 1925 and 1927, with the help of the Rockefeller family, the world church movement began. In 1948 this world church movement was officially organized as the

World Council of Churches. Since its very inception, the World Council of Churches has consisted primarily of those churches that have strayed from upholding the truths of the Bible, and the movement has been opposed by the evangelical churches.

Revelation 17:1–6 describes a "woman sitting on a scarlet beast" with the words "MYSTERY, BABYLON THE GREAT, THE MOTHER OF HARLOTS AND OF THE ABOMINATIONS OF THE EARTH." The great harlot is Babylon and is often thought of as the ancient city of Rome. This is also symbolic of the coming counterfeit world church movement, which will promote a false religion. This false religion will help the Anti-christ gain control of the people and will also persecute true believers in Jesus Christ.

Revelation 17:6 states, "I saw the woman, drunk with the blood of saints and with the blood of the martyrs of Jesus." An apostate church that denies the truth of the Word of God will eventually become the agency that will persecute and murder Christian believers. Many liberal churches today promote abortion and euthanasia. It is not hard to imagine that some day these churches will take the next step, which will be persecuting and even killing true Christian believers.

As an example of how far some denominations have strayed from their biblical beginnings, the Presbyterian church (USA) gathered with feminist leaders from the World Council of Churches to "destroy patriarchal religion" and worship the goddess Sophia. At the four-day event, they even went so far as to affirm lesbian lovemaking. And, during the conference, Arunda Gnanadason of the World Council of Churches condemned the Christian church for centering its faith on the death of Christ on the cross.

Melanie Morrison of CLOUT (Christian Lesbians Out Together) invited all the lesbian, bisexual, and transsexual women to come forward and celebrate their lesbian relationships. Clearly, the World Council of Churches and some of the liberal denominations that it represents have rejected the worship of Jesus Christ for idols of their own making. Like the children of Israel in Moses' time, they are dancing around a golden calf in defiance of the true God. Unfortunately, this is not an isolated event; many of these churches have openly homosexual pastors and advocate homosexuality, abortion, the occult, and other practices not pleasing to God.

A Firsthand Encounter with Truth

I did not grow up in a religious home. I was raised in New York City where my parents were both humanists and basically raised me to believe that Christianity was a religion for ignorant, uneducated, and superstitious people. However, at a young age, I sensed a deep spiritual vacuum within me and began a spiritual quest that lasted for two decades. As a teen-ager, I became involved in meditation, Hinduism, Buddhism, the study of psychology, and a variety of Eastern mystical religions.

While studying at the University of Missouri, my major was the brand new experimental field of psychology called "Altered States of Consciousness," in which we studied the teachings of the gurus, practiced meditation, and examined Eastern religious practices from a so-called scientific perspective. During this spiritual search, I experienced first hand things like seeing "The Great White Light" and entering realms of higher consciousness.

After reading a book called *Heaven and Hell and the Doors of Perception* by Aldous Huxley, I began using psychedelic drugs like mescaline, LSD, and MDA to "expand" my mind. I practiced the teachings of Baba Ram Dass, who taught psychology with Dr. Timothy Leary at Harvard; Carlos Castenedas; Stephen Gaskin, the American guru who founded the Farm commune; and tried some of the experiments in altered states of consciousness outlined by Dr. John C. Lilly about whose life the movie *The Day of Dolphin* was made. Lilly moved from studying the behavior of dolphins to immersing himself

in a sensory deprivation chamber, taking megadoses of
LSD, and leaving his body to communicate with "spirit
guides."

I was also involved in radical politics and wanted to
see the American form of government merge into some
kind of one-world government. During this time, I ran
into people of the Jesus movement on the campus of the
University of Missouri. They challenged me to consider
the claims of Jesus Christ and read books by people like
Dr. Francis Schaeffer. I was shocked to discover that
Christians could be intelligent, and that Dr. Schaeffer
could give a brilliant intellectual defense of the Christian
faith.

One day I was invited to a Christian religious retreat
about an hour outside of the campus of the University of
Missouri. When I got there, it confirmed my worst fears
about Christianity. I went there looking for reality and
ran into a bunch of people with a "country club" religion
that had no reality. I was totally disgusted and decided to
hitchhike back to the campus.

A series of small miracles happened to me on the way
back to the university. After being told by the guy who
invited me to the religious retreat that God would take
care of my rides home, I was mysteriously picked up by
a First Pentecostal preacher and his wife, who shared the
Gospel of Jesus Christ with me. Then, my second ride
was from a Bible salesman with a station wagon filled with
Bibles. This Bible salesman led me in the sinner's prayer
where I invited Jesus Christ to forgive me of my sins and
make me born again.

The next day I had an overwhelming experience where
I knew that Jesus Christ was really God and that all of
these Eastern mystical experiences were false and illu-
sory. For the first time in my life, I knew that I had really
found God. Then, slowly after studying the Bible, my
lifestyle began to radically change. I began to understand
that the God of the Bible really exists and that He has a
plan for each man and woman, as well as the human race.

I realized that many of the things that I had been educated to believe were simply not true, and my personal encounter with Jesus Christ had a profound effect on my political world view, my morals, and my spiritual belief system. I understood that man was not the product of some evolutionary accident or random mixture of primordial ooze; man was placed here by specific design by an omnipotent Creator, and this Creator has a passionate love for each person who ever lived.

Receiving Jesus Christ into my life was the single most liberating and revolutionary thing I had ever done in my life. Far from being some "blind leap of faith," my decision to accept Christ into my life was the most pragmatically rational thing I had ever done. It has placed me on the most wondrous and amazing journey that a person can have.

Chapter Twenty-two

The Biography of Satan

You cannot understand biblical prophecy unless you understand that there is a devil and that he has a game plan in what the Bible calls the last days. Starting in the Garden of Eden when the serpent deceived Adam and Eve and brought about the Fall of the human race, there has been a struggle between good and evil in our world. In Ezekiel 28:12–16 we learn about the king of Tyre, who is in reality Satan.

> You were the seal of perfection, full of wisdom and perfect in beauty. You were in Eden, the garden of God; every precious stone was your covering: the sardius, topaz, and diamond, beryl, onyx, and jasper, sapphire, turquoise, and emerald with gold. The workmanship of your timbrels and pipes was prepared for you on the day you were created. You were the anointed cherub who covers; I established you; you were on the holy mountain of God; you walked back and forth in the midst of the fiery stones. You were perfect in your ways from the day you were created, till iniquity was found in you. By the abundance of your trading you became filled with violence within, and you sinned; therefore I cast you as a profane thing out of the mountain of God; and I destroyed you, O covering cherub, from the midst of the fiery stones.

Here we get to read Satan's job résumé. Satan once was God's right-hand angel who was beautiful and had the "seal of perfection." In fact, Satan used to be "the anointed cherub who covers," meaning that he was in charge of covering and protecting the holy mountain of God. Verse thirteen teaches us that Satan, or Lucifer, was in charge of leading heaven's choirs in worship to God. It is no accident that today certain forms of music have the power to corrupt mankind with sex, violence, Satanism, and drugs. The devil is a musical being and understands how the power of music can sway the human soul.

Satan is also the ultimate business executive. In verse sixteen we read that this king of Tyre became filled with violence because of the abundance of his trading. This present world economic system is being controlled by Satan and his principalities and powers. In Revelation 18:1–24 we see the Babylonian, or world, economic system coming to an end. It is no accident that the road to one-world government, global immorality, and the persecution of God's people is driven by the financial institutions of this world. Jesus Christ referred to this when He warned His followers that "you cannot serve God and mammon" (Luke 16:13). Mammon is more than just money; it refers to the spirit behind the world economic system, which Satan controls.

Although money is not intrinsically evil, the love of money, which dominates the world economic system, is the tool Satan uses to control the world. Make no mistake about it; the spiritual root of this present global economic system is not based on God but on a total lust for money and power, which is a form of worship of mammon and Satan.

Selling Your Soul to the Devil

Satan is the great counterfeiter. Just as God searches the hearts of men and seeks to find men and women who will yield themselves as intercessors to the Holy Spirit (Ezek. 22:30), Satan goes about the earth seeking men whom he can seduce for his dark purposes. Aleister Crowley, who was the self-proclaimed Beast 666, was an infamous English Satanist who has influenced many people in our world from rock musicians to cult leaders. Crowley wrote the Satanist book, *The Book of the Law*, whose theme was "Do what thou will shall be the whole of the Law." In a sense, this is the basic commandment of Satan and the total opposite of God's laws which are based on love. "Do what thou will" is the Satanic commandment of self-satisfaction at any price.

Aleister Crowley's Satanic law is really a repeat of Satan's mistake of asserting his will rather than God's in Isaiah 14:12–14, in which Satan says in his heart, "I will be like the Most High." Aleister Crowley, who lived in Tunbridge Wells, England, had a profound influence on rock 'n' roll groups like the Beatles, who had his picture on the cover of their *Sergeant Pepper's Lonely Hearts Club Band* album, and on groups like Ozzie Osborne, the Red Hot Chili Peppers, and Led Zeppelin. The drummer of Led Zeppelin bought and lived in Crowely's English estate, and one of the songs of the Red Hot Chili Peppers is called "Sex Magick," which was one of Crowley's occult practices.

Aleister Crowley, who was raised in a Christian home, rejected his upbringing and decided in his teens that he was the Beast in the Book of Revelation. Crowley was an artist, explorer, drug user, and practicer of Buddhism, Taoism, Yoga, and magick. His teachings influenced the Nazis and continue to be spread all over the world today. Crowley in his book, *Magick in Theory and Practice*, spelled the word magic with a *K* to make it distinct from the ordinary magic practiced by all kinds of people: Aleister Crowley's magick was based on Satanism.

Aleister Crowley taught and practiced what many people secretly believe today, and that is that if they give their lives over to the devil, that Satan will give them supernatural power. Although Aleister Crowley was not the Beast in the Book of Revelation, the time is coming when men and women will give their allegiance to the true Beast of Revelation. Already, there are people alive

in our world today who are deliberately yielding themselves to become instruments of the powers of darkness
as men like Adolf Hitler and Aleister Crowley did. Perhaps, somewhere in the world today, the real Anti-christ
may be yielding his mind and personality to Satan so that
he can become the Anti-christ of Revelation.

The point is that all of us choose either consciously or
unconsciously whether or not we will serve Christ or the
devil. There are men and women alive today who may
never admit that they are worshipping Satan, but, in their
hearts, they have decided to do anything to anyone if it
will serve their lust for power, money, position, and fame.
In reality, they are following in Satan's footsteps when he
asserted his will and not God's, or Crowley's dictum of
"Do what thou wilt."

We mistakenly think of Satan worshippers as having
long hair and beards with a pentagram hanging around
their neck. But, there are men and women in the great
corporations of our world, the entertainment industry,
and politics who have become absolutely ruthless in their
quest for power. In their inner being, they have said, "My
will" and not God's, and they have followed the dictum,
"Do what thou wilt." In reality, on some deep inner level,
they have chosen to become servants of Satan.

The evidences of this kind of spiritual corruption are
everywhere from the corporate giants who manufacture
food knowing full well it is giving people cancer, to the
politicians who have sold our nation down the river for
money, to the record and movie producers who have
corrupted our youth for the sake of money. It is a chilling
thought to think that there are people who would deliberately follow Satan and not God. But, the Bible says that
this is what is really going on.

The Story of Lucifer

The prophet Isaiah gives us some remarkable insight
into why Lucifer, or Satan, fell from his exalted position
to become the devil. Here we see that Lucifer's big mis-

take was wanting to be God and that he wanted his will instead of God's will:

> How you are fallen from heaven, O Lucifer, son of the morning! How you are cut down to the ground, you who weakened the nations! For you have said in your heart: I will ascend into heaven, I will exalt my throne above the stars of God; I will also sit on the mount of the congregation on the farthest sides of the north; I will ascend above the heights of the clouds, I will be like the Most High. Yet, you shall be brought down to Sheol, to the lowest depths of the Pit. Those who see you will gaze at you, and consider you saying: "Is this the man who made the earth tremble, who shook kingdoms, who made the world as a wilderness and destroyed its cities, who did not open the house of his prisoners?" (Isa. 14:12–17)

Lucifer fell from heaven because he wanted to do his will rather than God's will and he wanted to be God. Ironically, this is the same sin that many people in our society have fallen into because, in a vain attempt to be masters of their own destiny, they really want to be God. Many people in the New Age movement and the Eastern religions are teaching people that, when they raise their consciousness high enough, they will discover that they are God. Stewart Brand, who founded the *Whole Earth Catalog*, coined the expression, "Since we are gods we may as well get good at it" (*The Millennium Whole Earth Catalog*, ed. Howard Rheingold [Harper San Francisco: HarperCollins, New York, 1995], 1). The idea is that man is God, which is total deception.

Whenever a person desires his or her own will rather than God's will, they are following in the steps of Lucifer's rebellion. In the end, Lucifer is going to be banished to the bottomless pit and hell where all those who reject God's message of salvation by faith in Jesus Christ are going to spend eternity. In Revelation 20:1–3, we are told that Satan's residence is the bottomless pit:

Then I saw an angel coming down from heaven, having the key to the bottomless pit and a great chain in his hand. He laid hold of the dragon, that serpent of old, who is the Devil and Satan, and bound him for a thousand years; and he cast him into the bottomless pit, and shut him up, and set a seal on him, so that he should deceive the nations no more till the thousand years were finished. But after these things he must be released for a little while.

Lucifer's destiny is to be defeated by Jesus Christ and to be banished to the bottomless pit and the lake of fire. Revelation 20:10 states, "The devil, who deceived them, was cast into the lake of fire and brimstone where the beast and the false prophet are. And they will be tormented day and night forever and ever." In these last days Satan knows that his days are numbered, and he is unleashing all kinds of deception upon the people of the world. In Revelation 12:12, John warns us, "Therefore rejoice, O heavens, and you who dwell in them! Woe to the inhabitants of the earth and to the sea! For the devil has come down to you, having great wrath, because he knows that he has a short time."

The Satanic Rebellion

Many years ago, Satan led a rebellion against God in the spiritual realm, or invisible world. In fact, one third of all the angels in heaven have revolted against God and are following Satan's orders. This is why in our day of such a great resurgence of interest in the subject of angels, it is important to understand that there are good as well as bad angels and not all angels are from God. In Revelation 12:4, 9 we read an account of this Satanic rebellion:

His tail drew a third of the stars of heaven and threw them to the earth. And the dragon stood before the woman who was ready to give birth, to devour the Child as soon as it was born. . . . So the

great dragon was cast out, that serpent of old, called
the Devil and Satan who deceives the whole world;
he was cast to the earth, and his angels were cast
out with him.

Our world is filled with demonic powers that are
waging war against mankind at every level. The current
rise in the occult with all the increased interest in channeling, psychics, astrology, the New Age, drugs, Satanism,
witchcraft, and occult religions stems from Satan's revolution against God and demon activity.

Chapter Twenty-three

The Cosmic Switch

At a certain time, which is only known to God, the God of the universe is going to trip a kind of cosmic switch in the invisible realm, and the Church of Jesus Christ is going to be raptured from the planet. It is going to be a mind-blowing event as millions of Christians leave the planet before a time of great trouble prophesied by the prophet Jeremiah. The people who are left here on earth are going to have to come up for an explanation as to why millions of Christians have suddenly disappeared. Perhaps, they are going to adopt the New Age view that the earth has been "cleansed," or that these Christians have been forcibly removed by aliens before the dawn of a New Age of harmony and peace for mankind.

It is going to be an event with more special effects than any science fiction film ever made, as believers are supernaturally caught up with Jesus Christ. Our modern world, which is so locked into its so-called rationalistic and scientific viewpoint, is going to be completely thrown for a loop when the Rapture occurs. The Rapture is going to be as miraculous as the creation of Adam and Eve, the parting of the Red Sea, Noah being rescued in an ark, and the death and resurrection of Jesus Christ.

In the *Star Trek* films and television series, the old expression was "beam me up, Scotty." Captain Kirk and even the next generation of *Star Trek* heroes were beamed up to the Starship Enterprise as an advanced form of transportation. God is far ahead of the writers of *Star Trek*. He planned to "beam" His people up before the beginning of time.

However, the people who are alive on earth are going to have to have to come up with some pretty strong rationalizations, excuses, and denials when this event happens. The Rapture is going to kick off a series of cataclysmic changes on the planet when the Anti-christ takes over, the Great Tribulation begins, and Armageddon goes down. It is literally going to be the beginning of the end of this world as we know it and the dawn of eternity.

The Rapture

Although the exact word *rapture* does not occur in the Bible, 1 Thessalonians 4:17 gives us the main passage where this biblical truth is taught: "Then we who are alive and remain shall be caught up together with them in the clouds to meet the Lord in the air. And thus we shall always be with the Lord." The phrase "caught up" comes from the Greek word *harpadzo*, which means to seize, snatch away, catch up, or take up by force. This same word describes when the Holy Spirit transfers Philip the evangelist to Azotus in Acts 8:39–40.

The word *rapture* came from a Latin translation of the Bible, which said, *rapiemur cum illis*, which means caught up together with Him, or rapture. Although there is debate among equally sincere Christians as to the exact timing of the Rapture, the Rapture is a solid biblical doctrine and one which every Christian should look forward to.

The Apostle Paul explains in 1 Thessalonians 4:13–18:

> But, I do not want you to be ignorant, brethren, concerning those who have fallen asleep, lest you sorrow as others who have no hope. For if we believe that Jesus died and rose again, even so God will bring with Him those who sleep in Jesus. For this we say to you by the word of the Lord, that we

who are alive and remain until the coming of the
Lord will by no means precede those who are asleep.
For the Lord Himself will descend from heaven
with a shout, with the voice of an archangel, and
with the trumpet of God. And the dead in Christ
will rise first. Then those who are alive and remain
shall be caught up together with them in the clouds
to meet the Lord in the air. And thus we shall
always be with the Lord. Therefore comfort one
another with these words.

The Apostle Paul does not want God's people to be ignorant of the reality of the Rapture. In fact, we are to "comfort one another" (v. 18) with this truth. It should be of
great comfort to believers in Jesus that there is coming a
time when we are getting out of here. Let's face it: planet
earth is a mess, and God is going to rescue His people
and rapture them to live with Him forever in heaven.

When this event happens, the dead in Christ will rise
first, and then the living will follow them into heaven (1
Thess. 4:13). However, intelligent and equally committed
believers disagree as to the timing of key prophetic events
in Scripture, such as the Rapture, the Great Tribulation,
and the emergence of the Anti-christ. Perhaps the most
popular viewpoint is the pretribulation rapture position,
which teaches that the Rapture will precede the seven-
year tribulation on earth. There is the Premillennial
Prewrath Rapture view, which teaches that believers will
be raptured three and a half years in the Great Tribulation before the wrath of God is poured out. However,
other people believe the Church will go through the Tribulation with Jesus.

Bible prophecy expert and business executive Chuck
Missler, who is a strong pretribulationist, adds an interesting comment,

Many of us hold to a "pre-trib" rapture—I sure
do—but there is a serious "risk" in misapplying this
viewpoint. There is a tendency for many Christians
to assume that we will be "snatched out" before any

troubles begin. It is perhaps naive (and dangerous!) for us to presume that we will be "raptured" instead of having to endure the apparent disasters of which this country may be heir. "Rapture-itis" seems a peculiarly American presumption. (Many of you may not believe in a pre-tribulational rapture. Don't worry about it we will explain it to you on the way up.) Just because we understand that the church will be removed before that specific period of time known as "The Great Tribulation" doesn't mean we are immune to times of serious persecution and troubles." (Chuck Missler, *Personal Update* [September 1994])

America is walking on very thin ice in terms of facing the consequences of its gross immorality, sin, and political failures. Our trillion dollar debt and rejection of Judeo-Christian values is going to reap a bitter harvest if we do not see repentance and revival. However, God is committed by a covenant to His people, and He is not going to pour out punishment on those who love and obey Him. The Bible is filled with examples of how God supernaturally delivers His covenant people. Moses led the Jewish people supernaturally out of the evil clutches of Pharaoh. Noah and his family were miraculously delivered by an ark. Daniel was divinely protected from the fiery furnace and the lion's den. Joseph was rescued out of slavery, and there are countless examples of God's deliverance and mercy.

However, this does not mean that believers will not have to face persecution, difficulty, imprisonment, and even death. Our responsibility as believers is to be filled with His Holy Spirit and walk daily with Jesus Christ. We are to trust God completely in good times and bad. The Apostle Paul said, "I know how to be abased, and I know how to abound. Everywhere in all things I have learned both to be full and to be hungry, both to abound and to suffer need. I can do all things through Christ who strengthens me" (Phil. 4:12–13).

Christianity is not fatalism. We are never to sit passively by and watch our nation surrender to the powers of darkness. We can look forward confidently to the Rapture of the Church while we reclaim our nation for Jesus Christ. For the sake of our children and grandchildren we must fast, pray, evangelize, and participate in the democratic process.

The "blessed hope" does not mean that American Christians are never going to experience trials, adversity, persecution, and the like. God is going to supernaturally deliver His people before the Great Tribulation, but there may be days of great difficulty ahead as we approach this period. This is why it is so important to every Christian to be committed to praying, fasting, and evangelizing before the Rapture of the Church and to participate in the political process while we still have the freedom to do so. Jesus Christ commanded us to occupy until He comes.

Out of Here

There are numerous passages of Scripture that seem to suggest that believers in Jesus Christ will not be around for the Anti-christ and the seven-year tribulation period known as the Time of Jacob's Trouble. First Thessalonians 5:9 states, "For God did not appoint us to wrath, but to obtain salvation through our Lord Jesus Christ." And, Revelation 3:10 states, "Because you have kept My command to persevere, I will keep you from the hour of trial which shall come upon the whole world, to test those who dwell on the earth." This reads in the Amplified Bible, "I also will keep you [safe] from the hour of trial [testing] which is coming on the whole world." The Living Bible states, "I will protect you from the time of the Great Tribulation and Temptation, which will come upon the world." The idea communicated here is that the Church of Jesus Christ will be raptured before this time of testing and the Great Tribulation.

Once again, although we may look forward to being raptured and delivered, our emphasis should be on being the people who God created us to be and doing what God commanded us to do. This means that as believers in Jesus Christ we should be living pure and holy lives and are to be filled with His Holy Spirit. God has placed each of us here on this earth to minister the life and reality of Jesus Christ to others. This is where our focus should be.

In addition, although we may speculate concerning last days events, we must humbly remember that the times and seasons are in God's hands. As such, we must conduct our lives with the utmost wisdom, plan for the future, and do everything that we can to give a future worth living in to our children. If we simply let go in a kind of fatalism and allow our nation and world to be surrendered into the hands of evil people, our children will experience horrible persecution, and their lives will be agonizingly painful.

Although we may look with anticipation for the Rapture, we must remember that Proverbs 12:24 states, "The hand of the diligent will rule, But the lazy man will be put to forced labor," or, as one translation reads, "the slothful shall be under tribute." Apathetic, fatalistic, lazy, and slothful people will be ruled by oppressors. This is not God's will for our children. If we love our children we will pray, intercede, evangelize, participate in the political process, and stand up and be counted for righteousness as never before, while there is still time.

The UFO Conspiracy

Not too long ago, I was lying on my back in the backyard with my wife and son at night looking up at the stars. We were out there to watch a meteor shower that looked like a kind of cosmic pinball machine as shooting stars streaked across the sky. Then, out of the corner of my eye, I saw this dark object move across the night sky. It seemed to slide across the sky about twice the speed of a jet, and it was totally silent. Whenever we see jets fly above our home, we always here the roar of a jet engine, but this thing was totally silent.

I was tempted to think it was a UFO, but I don't really believe there are aliens flying around from another planet. That isn't to say that I don't believe that UFOs are real; it's just that I have another explanation that I will get into in a minute. I believe that this thing flying above my house was some kind of Stealth jet that was painted black and had the ability to fly very quickly and silently across the sky. It looked as if it was headed towards Edwards Airforce Base out in the desert.

I know a lot of people believe in UFOs, and movies like *Communion* and *Fire in the Sky* popularize the belief. However, I have a different opinion about aliens and UFOs. First of all, I think there are just far too many accounts of people encountering aliens and reporting being abducted by spacecraft to dismiss the whole thing as nonsense. I believe that these people are encountering beings from another world, but that these beings are not aliens in the true sense of the word, but demons.

I think that Satan is sending his demons out in an all-out effort to deceive people. It's interesting to note that many of the people who have reported encounters with aliens have had involvement in occult activities. Best-selling author Whitley Streiber, who wrote *Communion* and *Transformation*, which details his encounters with UFOs and aliens, was deeply involved in the occult for years before he had these experiences. Many of the people who have encountered UFOs and aliens have been fooling around with the occult before they had these experiences.

I believe that all occult involvement no matter how subtle or innocent can open the door, even if it is just a crack, to the demonic realm. People who dabble with Eastern meditation, astrology, channeling, drugs, hypnosis, past life regression, Tarot cards, and other occult oriented activities have inadvertently opened the door in the invisible realm and have given the powers of darkness a foothold in their lives.

It could be that Satan is very subtly preparing the people of earth for some kind of powerful deception in

which aliens will give the human race some kind of supernatural guidance. It is interesting to note that every single
message given by an alien totally contradicts the gospel of
Jesus Christ and sets up a counterfeit gospel. Some have
suggested that the Anti-christ will use UFOs as the explanation as to why millions of Christians have disappeared
from earth in the Rapture. Whatever the case, UFOs and
aliens are clearly the product of deceiving spirits who are
out to blind men and women from the gospel of Jesus
Christ.

Chapter Twenty-four

The False Prophet

In Revelation 13:11, we are introduced to "another beast coming up out of the earth." This second beast with "horns like a lamb" and who speaks like a dragon is the False Prophet. The False Prophet is part of Satan's counterfeit Trinity that consists of Satan, the Anti-christ, and the False Prophet. Although, the False Prophet will pose as a true prophet, he will be a deceiver. This False Prophet will have tremendous supernatural power to perform great signs and to call fire down from heaven in order to deceive mankind.

The job of the False Prophet will be to cause people to worship the Anti-christ. Interestingly enough, it is not the Anti-christ who will be specifically responsible for making people accept the mark of the Beast. It is the False Prophet who will be assigned the task of causing people to take the mark of the Beast, which will be related to the number 666.

At this time in human history, the occult power of deception will be increased. Just like Adolf Hitler, who was deeply involved in the occult, both the Anti-christ and the False Prophet will have tremendous occult power. I believe that at this time in history, all the occult, Eastern mystical, and other religions will be united into one false world religion by the False Prophet.

The current move to unite the world's religions will come to its fruition when the False Prophet arises. Astrology, channeling, meditation, drugs, ESP, altered states of consciousness, Hinduism, Buddhism, Islam, the New Age, and many other religious teachings will be finally unified by the False Prophet into a great one-world religion.

If you examine the recent developments in the New Age movement or the Higher Consciousness movement in which I used to be deeply involved and wrote about in a number of my earlier books like *Who Will Rule the Future? A Resistance to the New World Order, Evangelizing the New Age and Supernatural Faith in the New Age,* you will discover that all the channelers, psychics, gurus, astrologers, and spiritual teachers keep talking about a coming time of global unity and a new golden age. In fact, the people who claim to have been visited by UFOs also claim that aliens have told them to get ready for a new era in mankind's history where the world will be united as one. I believe that all of these ideas are being injected into the minds of people by demonic entities who are preparing the world for the worship of the Anti-christ.

Satan Is Bound for One Thousand Years

Ever since the Garden of Eden when the "serpent of old" seduced Adam and Eve, Satan has been creating problems for mankind. Now finally, an angel is going to come from heaven, after Satan is defeated at Armageddon, and lock him up in a supernatural bottomless pit for a thousand years: "Then I saw an angel coming down from heaven, having the key to the bottomless pit and a great chain in his hand. He laid hold of the dragon, that serpent of old who is Devil and Satan, and bound him for a thousand years" (Rev. 20:2–3).

Tragically, there are growing numbers of young people who think it is fashionable to worship Satan and have become Satanists. If you watch MTV or look at the covers of compact discs featuring prominent rock 'n' roll groups, you will see all kinds of occult and Satanic imagery. When I have spoken across the nation at conventions, universities, and churches, I will often meet people who tell me about the rise of witchcraft and Satan worship among the young people in their communities. But, Revelation 20:1–3 reveals that Satan's destiny is to be bound up and thrown in a bottomless pit for a thousand years, and then he is going to be cast into the lake of fire forever: "The devil, who deceived them, was cast into the lake of fire and brimstone where the beast and the false prophet are. And they will be tormented day and night forever and ever" (Rev. 20:10). This Prince of Darkness is going to be damned for all eternity along with all those who have loved the darkness rather than the Light.

In our time, there is a tremendous fascination and obsession with evil, violence, perversion, degradation, and corruption. For example, billions of people worldwide have stayed glued to the O.J. Simpson trial, perhaps in order to watch computer animation reenactments of the savage murder. And, house guest Kato Kaelin has even become a kind of cult hero in this perverse drama.

Books, movies, and television programs about rape, murder, incest, molestation, torture, brutality, lust, seduction, greed, and manipulation are devoured by hungry audiences from New York City to Peking, China. Yet, the temporary ruler of this dark world is going to go down hard along with all those who have followed him.

Christ on a White Horse

Revelation 19:11 states, "Now I saw heaven opened, and behold a white horse. And He who sat on him was called Faithful and True, and in righteousness He judges and makes war." At the climax of Armageddon, Jesus Christ is going to return with His glorified saints in heaven and His angels to destroy the forces of the Beast. Jesus Christ will fight for Israel, and the military forces of the Beast and the False Prophet along with the armies of the kings of earth will be crushed by Jesus Christ. The white horse that Jesus Christ will ride symbolizes victory. Revelation 19:13 states, "He was clothed with a robe dipped in blood, and His name is called The Word of God." What this means is that when Jesus Christ returns, His robe will be dipped in the blood that He shed as a sacrifice for the sins of mankind. Yet, a sinful and rebellious mankind will ignore His sacrificial death and join the Anti-christ in this final battle against God.

Fallen mankind who has willfully chosen to follow the Anti-christ are going to wage war against Jesus Christ and the armies of heaven: "And I saw the beast, the kings of the earth, and their armies, gathered together to make war against Him who sat on the horse and against His army" (Rev. 19:19). The armies in heaven, which are the saints of God who have been cleansed by the blood of the Lamb and who are "clothed in fine linen, white and clean, followed Him on white horses" (Rev. 19:14).

This is going to be an awesome sight as Jesus Christ comes out of the sky riding a white horse with the saints of God also riding white horses charging into battle against the armies of the Beast. It is going to be a war that is more fantastic than any science fiction movie ever produced. The literal sky is going to light up as Jesus Christ and the armies of heaven ride down to the earth.

At this time, Jesus Christ and His armies are going to capture the Beast, False Prophet, and everyone who chose to receive the mark of the Beast and who worshipped his image. The Beast and the False Prophet are literally going to be cast alive into the lake of fire, which burns with brimstone (Rev. 19:20–21). In stark contrast, to the wondrous and joyous marriage supper of the Lamb, birds of prey are going to feast on the flesh of those who chose to reject Christ and follow the Beast. This will be more hideous than anything horror novelist Stephen King has ever written.

"Then I saw an angel standing in the sun; and he cried with a loud voice, saying to all the birds that fly in the midst of heaven, Come and gather together for the supper of the great God, that you may eat the flesh of kings, the flesh of captains, the flesh of mighty men, the flesh of horses and of those who sit upon them, and the flesh of all people, free and slave, both small and great"

(Rev. 19:18). God is going to allow these birds of prey to devour His enemies. Now, if you think God is being cruel and unjust in allowing this to happen, you must remember that these people hate truth, righteousness, love, purity, holiness, and Jesus Christ. They have become totally perverse and corrupt and are worthy of destruction.

Welcome to the Millennium

As the expression goes, "If you remember the sixties, you probably weren't there." Well, like many of you I lived through the sixties and early seventies, and, despite all the drugs and partying, I remember it—well some of it anyway. But, originally the sixties was about ushering in a new era of love, peace, and brotherhood. Rock festivals like Woodstock and more recently Woodstock II attempted to promote the idea of love, peace, and music. This counter-culture ideal of bringing mankind back to Paradise still lives on in the ecology movement and other activist groups.

However, the Bible speaks of a time when there will be a real millennium of a thousand years of peace, love, and brotherhood when man and nature will live in total harmony like it was back in the Garden of Eden. Isaiah 12:6–9 describes this future time when, "The wolf also shall dwell with the lamb, the leopard shall lie down with the young goat, the calf and the young lion and the fatling together; and a little child shall lead them. The cow and the bear shall graze; their young ones shall lie down together; and the lion shall eat straw like the ox. The nursing child shall play by the cobra's hole, and the weaned child shall put his hand in the viper's den. They shall not hurt or destroy in all My holy mountain. For the earth shall be full of the knowledge of the Lord as the waters cover the sea" (Isa. 11:6–9).

The Millennium is going to be a time of perfect ecological harmony where people treat each other with dignity and respect. Nobody wants a polluted environment, and all of us enjoy a walk in nature with the sun shining and flowers blooming. But, the real pollution is not environmental but spiritual. It is man's heart that has been polluted along with the environment. Only the blood of Jesus Christ has the power to cleanse the human heart.

In the Millennium, God's people, who have had their hearts cleansed, will live with Jesus Christ on the earth for a thousand years. This will be a time of God's one-world government where Jesus Christ will rule the nations under His leadership (Rev. 20:4). During this thousand-year period God's people will reign with Christ, and the earth will be a place of great harmony and beauty. There will be no wars, pollution, strife, nor racism.

God's One-World Government

We are in the greatest battle the world has ever known, and that is the battle for earth and the souls of mankind. In the last days of human history, Satan is mobilizing an all-out attempt to counterfeit God's coming kingdom and one-world government. If we go back to the beginning in the Garden of Eden, we see that it was God's planet all the time. However, Adam and Eve were seduced by evil, and the Fall of Man occurred. Ever since that time, God has been in the business of redeeming mankind through His blood covenant.

At the same time, Satan has been waging war against God and man by attempting to blind men and women from the reality of the saving knowledge of Jesus Christ. As part of his final plan, Satan is going to attempt to counterfeit God's one-world government and establish his own one-world government under the leadership of the Anti-christ.

This great movement towards a one-world government is the final fulfillment of man's disobedience to the Word of God that happened in the Garden of Eden. Yet, it will be crushed and exposed for exactly what it is, and that is an attempt to overthrow the very throne of God. Revelation 6:13 states, "Blessing and honor and glory and power Be to Him who sits on the throne, And to the

Lamb, forever and ever!" Jesus Christ is the "King of Kings and Lord of Lords" (Rev. 19:16).

This whole world system will be judged for what it is, and that is one gigantic smoke and mirrors show. Like the story in *The Wizard of Oz*, the Anti-christ is going to be exposed for who he is, and that is a false Christ. This entire world system that we live in that parades itself so proudly as enlightened, scientific, tolerant, and rational will be shown for what it really is, and that is a sham.

Ultimate truth and final reality will return to the human race as Jesus Christ returns to this world to set up His millennial kingdom. All the lies and arguments against God and His laws will appear ridiculous in the sight of His coming.

Chapter Twenty-five

A Spiritual Revolution, Not Political

In Acts 1:1–8, the physician Luke describes the transfer of Christ's authority and mission to His disciples. In verse six, the disciples are still thinking of the messianic kingdom in terms of political power: "Therefore, when they had come together, they asked Him, saying, 'Lord, will you at this time restore the kingdom to Israel?'" Jesus Christ answered them, saying, "It is not for you to know times or seasons which the Father has put in his own authority. But you shall receive power when the Holy Spirit has come upon you; and you shall be witnesses to Me in Jerusalem, and in all Judea and Samaria, and to the end of the earth" (Acts 1:7–8).

Jesus Christ was not talking about a political revolution but a spiritual one where His disciples were filled with power of the Holy Spirit, which comes from the Greek word *dunamis*, which means "energy, power, great force, great ability, and strength," from which we get our word *dynamite*. The disciples were called to be spiritual revolutionaries who overthrew the powers of darkness in the invisible realm through the power of the Holy Spirit.

This theme is continued in Ephesians 6:12, in which the Apostle Paul writes, "For we do not wrestle against flesh and blood, but against principalities, against powers, against rulers of darkness of this age, against spiritual hosts of wickedness in the heavenly places." Although the Christian must participate in the political process and be salt and light in the major power centers of our culture, our primary battle is spiritual, and our power comes from the *dunamis* of the Holy Spirit. If we are to truly transform our culture, then we are going to have to employ spiritual weapons. This does not mean that we are to retreat from active participation in politics, education, the media, the arts, and other fronts of the cultural war. For the sake of our children, we must show up and participate in the democratic process. However, we must not lose sight of the fact that the conflict is spiritual in origination.

Our battlefield is in the heavens, and our weapons are prayer, praise, fasting, and intercession. The invasion we launch must be against demonic powers and not people, who may be controlled by unseen forces. The banner we fly must be love, and the flag must be the bloodstained cross.

Warfare in the Invisible Realm

When we study biblical prophecy, history, or current events, it is impossible to really understand what is going on without acknowledging the fact that there is a spiritual realm that affects everything that is going on in the world. Governments, social movements, revivals, moral decay, and the fight between good and evil are all powerfully affected by a greater warfare that is going on in an invisible realm between God and Satan.

In Ephesians 6:10–12, the Apostle Paul outlines the nature of this battle in the invisible realm:

> Finally, my brethren, be strong in the Lord and in the power of His might. Put on the whole armor of God, that you may be able to stand against the wiles of the devil. For we do not wrestle against flesh and blood, but against principalities, against powers, against the rulers of the darkness of this age, against spiritual hosts of wickedness in the heavenly places.

Paul outlines this battle in the invisible realm for us to understand and explains to us that we are not fighting mere people but powerful beings in the spiritual world. The Church of Jesus Christ is not to be wrestling with human adversaries but principalities, powers, the rulers of the darkness of this age, and spiritual hosts of wickedness in the heavenly places. In other words, behind all of the social, political, and economic forces at work in our world today are spiritual forces.

Daniel 10:13 describes the battle between the senior angel Michael and the evil prince of Persia who was the head of the demonic forces in Persia. Daniel 10:20 describes the prince of Greece who is a powerful principality controlling the nation of Greece. Some people have labeled these evil spiritual beings territorial spirits, and there is evidence to suggest that many geographic locations in the world are being controlled by specific territorial spirits who are responsible for the spiritual climate of that region.

For example, in Hollywood, many people believe that one of the territorial spirits that control that area in California is a spirit of lust, which is evidenced in the sexual immorality that permeates the movies and television shows that are produced there. In Bogota, Columbia, a territorial spirit is behind the cocaine trade that is centered there; and in San Francisco, which is the head of the Satanist church, there are powerful spirits of witchcraft at work. The idea is not to get carried away and see a demon under every dinner plate, but to simply recognize that there is a real battle between the forces of good and evil in the invisible realm. Then, once you understand the nature of the warfare, you are to learn from the Bible how to engage in spiritual warfare with spiritual weapons. The purpose in reading about spiritual warfare is not to entertain you, but to equip you as a good soldier in Jesus Christ.

All Systems Go

We may well be on the verge of the final phase of human history. It would not take much for there to be major changes in the political landscape of our nation and world. If hyperinflation or a Great Depression happened in our nation, it would affect the whole earth like falling dominoes. If a nuclear weapon went off in a major city around the world as a result of a terrorist act, the world would be ready to accept the ideas of a powerful charismatic leader who promised the answers to world peace and economic prosperity.

However, I firmly believe we are in God's hands and that God has responded to the prayers, intercession, and fasting of His people who have called upon Him to move in our world. It is my opinion that we are in a season of God's grace where we are witnessing a tremendous outpouring of His Spirit throughout the earth. There are many things happening that offer tremendous rays of hope. For example, there are great signs of revival in major cities like Los Angeles, where hundreds of Christian leaders from a wide spectrum of denominations have gathered to pray for their city. This unity among Bible-believing evangelicals, fundamentalists, and charismatics is unprecedented.

There continues to be great thrusts of evangelism on the global level and in the United States. Millions of people are coming to Jesus Christ around the world. In America, there has been in recent years the rise of the Men's movement, launched by Coach McCartney, where millions of men who have rededicated their lives to God, their wives, and moral behavior, have packed stadiums across the country.

On the political landscape, there has been the widespread reentry of Christians who have chosen to participate in the political process, and there are great signs of positive change in our nation's government. Although we are in an era of all-out conflict between good and evil, there are many encouraging trends.

God's grace is being poured out on our land as He desires to bring people into His kingdom. John 3:16 states, "For God so loved the world that He gave His only begotten Son, that whoever believes in Him should not perish but have everlasting life." It is God's will to reach out to people and give them a chance to accept Jesus Christ as their personal Savior.

None of us knows how long this period of grace will be extended, and it would be very presumptuous of anyone to falsely assign a time to the Rapture or Second Coming. Each of us has a very deep responsibility to our children and the next generation to preserve our nation's freedom, to evangelize, and pray for the lost, for we do not know when Jesus Christ is coming. "Watch therefore, for you do not know what hour your Lord is coming" (Matt. 24:42). "Therefore you also be ready, for the Son of Man is coming at an hour you do not expect" (Matt. 24:44).

Yet, we must remember that things can dramatically change in an instant. We must continue to plan for the future and invest in our children's lives knowing that at some point in the future, life may change dramatically. We may find ourselves raptured and in heaven with Jesus Christ. "Then we who are alive and remain shall be caught up together with them in the clouds to meet the Lord in the air. And thus we shall always be with the Lord" (I Thess. 4:17).

To receive Paul McGuire's free newsletter or to have Paul speak at your church, convention or seminar, write

Paul McGuire
P.O. Box 803001
Santa Clarita, CA 91380-3001

ORDER THESE HUNTINGTON HOUSE BOOKS

- *Anyone Can Homeschool*—Terry Dorian & Zan Peters Tyler
- *The Assault*—Dale A. Berryhill
- *Beyond Political Correctness*—David Thibodaux
- *The Best of HUMAN EVENTS*—Edited by James C. Roberts
- *Bleeding Hearts and Propaganda*—James R. Spencer
- *Can Families Survive in Pagan America?*—Samuel Dresner
- *Circle of Death*—Richmond Odom
- *Children No More*—Brenda Scott
- *Combat Ready*—Lynn Stanley
- *Conservative, American & Jewish*—Jacob Neusner
- *The Dark Side of Freemasonry*—Ed Decker
- *The Demonic Roots of Globalism*—Gary Kah
- *Do Angels Really Exist?*—David O. Dykes
- *En Route to Global Occupation*—Gary Kah
- *Everyday Evangelism*—Ray Comfort
- **Exposing the AIDS Scandal*—Dr. Paul Cameron
- *Freud's War with God*—Jack Wright, Jr.
- *Gays & Guns*—John Eidsmoe
- *Global Bondage*—Cliff Kincaid
- *Goddess Earth*—Samantha Smith
- *Health Begins in Him*—Terry Dorian
- *Heresy Hunters*—Jim Spencer
- *Hidden Dangers of the Rainbow*—Constance Cumbey
- *High-Voltage Christianity*—Michael Brown
- *High on Adventure*—Stephen Arrington
- *Homeless in America*—Jeremy Reynalds
- *How to Homeschool (Yes, You!)*—Julia Toto
- *Hungry for God*—Larry E. Myers
- *I Shot an Elephant in My Pajamas*—Morrie Ryskind w/ John Roberts
- **Inside the New Age Nightmare*—Randall Baer
- *A Jewish Conservative Looks at Pagan America*—Don Feder
- *Journey into Darkness*—Stephen Arrington
- *Kinsey, Sex and Fraud*—Dr. Judith A. Reisman & Edward Eichel
- *The Liberal Contradiction*—Dale A. Berryhill
- *The Media Hates Conservatives*—Dale A. Berryhill
- *New Gods for a New Age*—Richmond Odom
- *One Man, One Woman, One Lifetime*—Rabbi Reuven Bulka
- *Out of Control*—Brenda Scott
- *Outcome-Based Education*—Peg Luksik & Pamela Hoffecker
- *The Parched Soul of America*—Leslie Kay Hedger w/ Dave Reagan
- *Please Tell Me*—Tom McKenney
- *Political Correctness*—David Thibodaux
- *Resurrecting the Third Reich*—Richard Terrell
- *Revival: Its Principles and Personalities*—Winkie Pratney

*Available in Salt Series

Available at bookstores everywhere or order direct from:
Huntington House Publishers • P.O. Box 53788 • Lafayette, LA 70505

Call toll-free 1-800-749-4009.